The Ultimate
CIVIL WAR QUIZ BOOK

❧ THE LOCHLAINN SEABROOK COLLECTION ❧

Five-Star Books & Gifts From the Heart of the American South

The Ultimate
CIVIL WAR QUIZ BOOK

HOW MUCH DO YOU REALLY KNOW ABOUT AMERICA'S MOST MISUNDERSTOOD CONFLICT?

GENEROUSLY ILLUSTRATED BY THE AUTHOR, "THE VOICE OF THE TRADITIONAL SOUTH," COLONEL

LOCHLAINN SEABROOK

JEFFERSON DAVIS HISTORICAL GOLD MEDAL WINNER

Diligently Researched for the Elucidation of the Reader

2017

Sea Raven Press, Nashville, Tennessee, USA

THE ULTIMATE CIVIL WAR QUIZ BOOK

Published by
Sea Raven Press, Cassidy Ravensdale, President
Southern Books, Real History!
PO Box 1484, Spring Hill, Tennessee 37174-1484 USA
SeaRavenPress.com • searavenpress@gmail.com

1st SRP paperback edition, 1st printing: August 2017, ISBN: 978-1-943737-51-2
1st SRP hardcover edition, 1st printing: August 2017, ISBN: 978-1-943737-52-9

ISBN: 978-1-943737-51-2 (paperback)
Library of Congress Control Number: 2017951569

The Ultimate Civil War Quiz Book: How Much Do You Really Know About America's Most Misunderstood Conflict? by Lochlainn Seabrook. Includes an index, endnotes, and bibliographical references.

Front and back cover design and art, book design, layout, and interior art by Lochlainn Seabrook
All images, graphic design, graphic art, and illustrations copyright © Lochlainn Seabrook
Cover image: U.S. National Flag and C.S. Battle Flag
Portions of this book have been adapted from the author's other works

The views on the American "Civil War" documented in this book are those of the publisher.

The paper used in this book is acid-free and lignin-free. It has been certified by the Sustainable Forestry Initiative and the Forest Stewardship Council and meets all ANSI standards for archival quality paper.

PRINTED & MANUFACTURED IN OCCUPIED TENNESSEE, FORMER CONFEDERATE STATES OF AMERICA

DEDICATION

To those seeking the truth about the
War for Southern Independence

EPIGRAPH

"Sit down before fact like a little child, and be prepared to give up every preconceived notion, follow humbly wherever and to whatever abyss Nature leads, or you shall learn nothing."

T. H. HUXLEY (1825-1895)

CONTENTS

SEA RAVEN PRESS

THE WORLD'S #1 SOUTH-FRIENDLY BOOK PUBLISHER

Restoring Dixie's honor
Defending traditional Southern culture
Preserving authentic Confederate history
One book at a time!

Nashville, Tennessee

SeaRavenPress.com

NOTES TO THE READER

THE TWO MAIN POLITICAL PARTIES IN 1860

☛ In any study of America's antebellum, bellum, and postbellum periods, it is vitally important to understand that in 1860 the two major political parties—the Democrats and the newly formed Republicans—were the opposite of what they are today. In other words, the Democrats of the mid 19th Century were Conservatives, akin to the Republican Party of today, while the Republicans of the mid 19th Century were Liberals, akin to the Democratic Party of today.[1]

Thus the Confederacy's Democratic president, Jefferson Davis, was a Conservative (with libertarian leanings); the Union's Republican president, Abraham Lincoln, was a Liberal (with socialistic leanings).[2]

The author's cousin, Confederate Vice President and Democrat Alexander H. Stephens: a Southern Conservative.

This is why, in the mid 1800s, the conservative wing of the Democratic Party was known as "the States' Rights Party."[3]

Hence, the Democrats of the Civil War period referred to themselves as "conservatives," "confederates," "anti-centralists," or "constitutionalists" (the latter because they favored strict adherence to the original Constitution—which tacitly guaranteed states' rights—as created by the Founding Fathers), while the Republicans called themselves "liberals," "nationalists," "centralists," or "consolidationists" (the latter three because they wanted to nationalize the central government and consolidate political power in Washington, D.C.).[4]

Since this idea is new to most of my readers, let us further demystify it by viewing it from the perspective of the American Revolutionary War. If Davis and his conservative Southern constituents (the Democrats of 1861) had been alive in 1775, they would have sided with George Washington and the American colonists, who sought to secede from the tyrannical government of Great Britain; if Lincoln and his Liberal Northern constituents (the Republicans of 1861) had been alive at that time, they would have sided with King George III and the English monarchy, who sought to maintain the American colonies as possessions of the British Empire. It is due to this very comparison that Southerners often refer to their secession as the Second Declaration of Independence and the "Civil War" as the Second American Revolutionary War.

Without a basic understanding of these facts, the American "Civil War" will forever remain incomprehensible. For a full discussion of this topic see my book, *Abraham Lincoln Was a Liberal, Jefferson Davis Was a Conservative: The Missing Key to Understanding the American Civil War.*

THE TERM "CIVIL WAR"

☞ As I heartily dislike the phrase "Civil War," its use throughout this book (as well as in my other works) is worthy of explanation.

Today America's entire literary system refers to the conflict of 1861 using the Northern term the "Civil War," whether we in the South like it or not. Thus, as all book searches by readers, libraries, and retail outlets

The American "Civil War" was not a true civil war as Webster defines it: "A conflict between opposing groups of citizens of the *same* country." It was a fight between two individual countries; or to be more specific, two separate and constitutionally formed confederacies: the U.S.A. and the C.S.A.

are now performed online, and as all bookstores categorize works from this period under the heading "Civil War," book publishers and authors who deal with this particular topic have little choice but to use this term themselves. If I were to refuse to use it, as some of my Southern colleagues have suggested, few people would ever find or read my books.

Add to this the fact that scarcely any non-Southerners have ever heard of the names we in the South use for the conflict, such as the "War for Southern Independence"—or my personal preference, "Lincoln's War." It only makes sense then to use the term "Civil War" in most commercial situations, distasteful though it is.

We should also bear in mind that while today educated persons, particularly educated Southerners, all share an abhorrence for the phrase "Civil War," it was not always so. Confederates who lived through and even fought in the conflict regularly used the term throughout the 1860s, and even long after. Among them were Confederate generals such as Nathan Bedford Forrest, Richard Taylor, and Joseph E. Johnston, not to mention the Confederacy's vice president, Alexander H. Stephens.

Confederate General James Longstreet was just one of many Southern officials who referred to the conflict of 1861 as the "Civil War."

In 1895 Confederate General James Longstreet wrote about his military experiences in a work subtitled, *Memoirs of the Civil War in America.* Even the Confederacy's highest leader, President Jefferson Davis, used the term "Civil War,"[5] and in one case at least, as late as 1881—the year he wrote his brilliant exposition, *The Rise and Fall of the Confederate Government.*[6] Authors writing for *Confederate Veteran* magazine sometimes used the phrase well into the early 1900s,[7] and in 1898, at the Eighth Annual Meeting and Reunion of the United Confederate Veterans (the forerunner of today's Sons of Confederate Veterans), the following resolution was proposed: that from then on the Great War of 1861 was to be designated "the Civil War Between the States."[8]

A WORD ON EARLY AMERICAN MATERIAL

☛ In order to preserve the authentic historicity of the Revolutionary and Civil War periods, I have retained the original spellings, formatting, and punctuation of the early Americans I quote. These include such items as British-English spellings, long-running paragraphs, obsolete words, and various literary devices peculiar to the time. Bracketed words within quotes are my additions and clarifications, while italicized words within quotes are (where indicated) my emphasis.

PRESENTISM

☞ As a historian I view *presentism* (judging the past according to present day mores and customs) as the enemy of authentic history. And this is precisely why the Left employs it in its ongoing war against traditional American, conservative, and Christian values. By looking at history through the lens of modern day beliefs, they are

Judging our ancestors by our own standards is unfair, unjust, misleading, and unethical.

able to distort, revise, and reshape the past into a false narrative that fits their ideological agenda: the liberalization *and* Northernization of America, the enlargement and further centralization of the national government, and total control of American political, economic, and social power, the same agenda that Lincoln championed.

This book rejects presentism and replaces it with what I call *historicalism*: judging our ancestors based on the values of their own time. To get the most from this work the reader is invited to reject presentism as well. In this way—along with casting aside preconceived notions and the fake "history" churned out by our left-wing education system—the truth in this work will be most readily ascertained and absorbed.

LEARN MORE

☞ Lincoln's War on the American people and the Constitution can never be fully understood without a thorough knowledge of the South's perspective. As this book is only meant to be a brief introductory guide to these topics, one cannot hope to learn the complete story here. For those who are interested in additional material from Dixie's viewpoint, please see my comprehensive histories listed on page 2.

Keep Your Body, Mind, & Spirit Vibrating at Their Highest Level

YOU CAN DO SO BY READING THE BOOKS OF

SEA RAVEN PRESS

There is nothing that will so perfectly keep your body, mind, and spirit in a healthy condition as to think wisely and positively. Hence you should not only read this book, but also the other books that we offer. They will quicken your physical, mental, and spiritual vibrations, enabling you to maintain a position in society as a healthy erudite person.

KEEP YOURSELF WELL-INFORMED!

The well-informed person is always at the head of the procession, while the ignorant, the lazy, and the unthoughtful hang onto the rear. If you are a Spiritual man or woman, do yourself a great favor: read Sea Raven Press books and stay well posted on the Truth. It is almost criminal for one to remain in ignorance while the opportunity to gain knowledge is open to all at a nominal price.

We invite you to visit our Webstore for a wide selection of wholesome, family-friendly, well-researched, educational books for all ages. You will be glad you did!

Five-Star Books & Gifts From the Heart of the American South

SeaRavenPress.com

Warning

This book will expand your mind

INTRODUCTION

WHY SHOULD ANYONE CARE ABOUT the American Civil War today? After all, it was nothing more than a battle between Northern abolitionists and Southern slave owners. The North won. Slavery was abolished. The Union was preserved. Victorian history. What relevance could any of this have to the modern world?

If this version, the Yankee version, of the War was true it truly *would* be irrelevant. Unfortunately, it is as false as false can be.

The victors wrote the history of the conflict and revised, edited, redacted, and altered it as they went along, editorializing literally every aspect of the War, from who started it to its very purpose. No detail was too small to be reexamined and overhauled. Even battle descriptions and statistics were modified or even falsified. Why? What could possibly be the reason for reframing the entire War, remolding the minutia of each year of the struggle, then inserting this massive coverup into our history books?

For the same reason the winners of all wars rewrite authentic history: to justify their otherwise unjustifiable actions. And this can only be accomplished by casting themselves as the "good guys" and their enemies as the "bad guys."

Who were the victors in the War for Southern Independence? They were not merely Northerners, abolitionists, or Unionists, as we have been taught. This is just another fairy tale, one more deceptive piece of what I call "The Great Yankee Coverup."

This question is most easily answered by looking at the true nature of the War itself, for it was far from being a battle over slavery, a fight between the "righteous" North and the "evil" South. Let us examine the facts more closely.

It is almost completely unknown to the general public that America's two main political parties were reversed in the mid 1800s. In other words, the Republicans were Liberals and the Democrats were Conservatives. I am the first historian to bring this fact to light in relation to the Civil War. As a result it reads like science fiction to many people. After all, if it were true why is it not in our history books?

It is not in our history books because it was suppressed during the initial invention of The Great Yankee Coverup, which began even while the War was raging.

Since mainstream history books are nearly all written by Liberals, socialists, communists, and by anti-Americans in general, one should not expect the truth about the Civil War to be found within their pages. What one *should* expect is that the unscrupulous creators of fake news would also create fake history, particularly when it comes to the Great War of 1861. And this is precisely what Liberals have done. To this day they continue to annually churn out thousands of books, articles, blogs, films, and TV documentaries reenforcing the falsehoods, lies, and slander of The Great Yankee Coverup.

For them there is no shame in this. It just politics as usual for Left-wing coastal elites and their massive global network of propaganda tools: liberal schools and colleges, liberal educators, liberal university presses, liberal TV companies, liberal TV anchors, journalists, commentators, documentarians, and activists, liberal film companies, scriptwriters, producers, directors, and actors, liberal Internet and social media companies, liberal bloggers, professional liberal malcontents, protestors, and rioters, and so on.

Covering up the truth about the American Civil War as well is exactly what one would anticipate from such individuals. These are, after all, the modern political descendants of the aggressive, meddling, self-righteous Yankees who invaded the South in 1861, and physically forced their progressive ideologies on Dixie at the tip of a gun barrel.

If this seems confusing to you it is because you are a victim of The Great Yankee Coverup!

Here is what they intentionally leave out of our history books to prevent you from learning the truth.

During the Civil War period Conservatives went by the name "Democrats"—and they had been since the election of Andrew Jackson in 1828; Liberals at the time went by the name "Republicans"—and had been since 1854, the year progressives and socialists founded the Republican Party to replace the recently extinct Whig Party (the major Liberal party between 1834 and 1854).

Thus, former Whig Abraham Lincoln, the presidential choice of the Republican Party (Union) during the 1860 election, was a Liberal, while his Southern foe, Jefferson Davis, the presidential choice of the Democratic Party (Confederate) that same year, was a Conservative. It

was not until the election of 1896 (between Conservative William McKinley and Liberal William Jennings Bryan) that the two parties would become the ones we are so familiar with today. That year they switched platforms, the Republicans becoming Conservatives, the Democrats becoming Liberals.

This fact alone makes the American Civil War relevant, for from this we can see that the conflict was actually nothing more than a continuation of the age old battle between liberalism and conservatism, the same one that, for Americans, began in 1788 with the presidency of left-leaning George Washington (a Federalist), and continues today under the current president and the opposing major party.

In short, what you need to know is that the Southern Confederacy under Davis—though its members went by the name "Democrat"—was a conservative body fighting for personal freedom, small government, and the Constitution, and is the ancestor of today's Republican Party. The Northern Union under Lincoln—though its members went by the name "Republican"—was a liberal body fighting for federal control, large government, and progressive (and in many cases, socialistic) ideas and polices, and is the ancestor of today's Democratic Party.

That our two-party platform reversal has been left out of our history books—leading in turn to a host of basic misunderstandings and common misinterpretations—is one of the great educational crimes of the century. For without a knowledge of this most important fact the Civil War is nonsensical. Worse, it loses all significance to modern Americans.[9]

And yet this is just one of thousands of such facts that have been forgotten, suppressed, or revised under The Great Yankee Coverup.

The Ultimate Civil War Quiz Book discusses this, as well as dozens of additional facts about Lincoln's War on the Constitution and the American people in the form of the following question types: question and answer, true or false, multiple choice, and fill in the blank. These fascinating but essential truths are not taught in our schools and are ignored by the Liberal-controlled mainstream media, furnishing an ideal opportunity for the reader to both test his or her knowledge of the *real* War—that is, the one intentionally hidden by the anti-South movement—while receiving an education in the South's perspective of the conflict.

Why do I call my work the *ultimate* quiz book? Because, as noted, the American Civil War is completely incomprehensible without the knowledge this book contains. As it will fill in the many gaping holes left by the confusing and purposefully misleading fake history fabricated by anti-South Liberals (and uneducated Conservatives), the information given here is fundamental to perceiving the full story of the antebellum, bellum, and postbellum periods in a holistic and objective manner.

This is *real* history. Read, absorb, learn, and, most importantly, share. An educated public is vital to free government, the very type of government the Confederacy fought and died trying to preserve, and which the Union fought and died trying to destroy.

Lochlainn Seabrook
Nashville, Tennessee, USA
August 2017

ONE

SECESSION

QUESTION: Which large Western country was literally founded on secession?

ANSWER: The United States of America was formed in 1776 after seceding from Great Britain.[10]

QUESTION: Where does the word secession come from?

ANSWER: It derives from the Latin word *secessus,* which is the past participle of *secedere,*[11] an intransitive verb meaning "go outside," "withdraw," or "to rebel."[12]

MULTIPLE CHOICE: Secession is

A. a Southern word.

B. a Yankee word.

C. an American word.

D. a universal word.

ANSWER: D. The word secession was coined by the English in 1604,[13] and has been used internationally ever since.[14]

QUESTION: What important early American document could be called our "National Ordinance of Secession"?

ANSWER: The Declaration of Independence, which states: "Whenever any form of government becomes destructive of these ends, it is the right of the people to alter or to abolish it, and to institute new government, laying its foundation on such principles, and organizing its powers in such form, as to them shall seem most likely to effect their safety and happiness."[15]

TRUE OR FALSE: The Founding Fathers did not include secession in the operations of the government.

ANSWER: False. The Founders deliberately made secession a vital "ingredient in the original composition of the general government."[16]

TRUE OR FALSE: The right of secession is discussed in the U.S. Constitution.

ANSWER: False. There is no direct or specific mention of secession in the U.S. Constitution.[17]

William Rawle.

MULTIPLE CHOICE: The Founding Fathers did not mention secession in the Constitution because

A. they did not care about it.

B. it was so commonly discussed and understood at the time they did not think it necessary.

C. they were against the idea of secession.

D. it was too controversial.

ANSWER: B. According to the noted 19th-Century constitutional scholar William Rawle of Pennsylvania, secession, "though not expressed [in the Constitution], was mutually understood."[18] Likewise, Alexander H. Stephens of Georgia stated that the right of secession "was generally recognized in all parts of the Union during the earlier days of the Republic."[19] Thus, as it was common knowledge, it was not necessary to itemize it in the Constitution.

QUESTION: Why is the right of secession not mentioned in any early American documents?

ANSWER: We have already seen that secession was the very basis of the Declaration of Independence, and that as a right it was indeed referred to in that document. As for America's other significant 18th- and 19th-Century writings, while secession may not have always been openly discussed, as an integral aspect of states' rights it was emphatically implied by the usage of various political words, phrases, and ideas regarding sovereignty.

For example, in our first Constitution, the Articles of Confederation (1781), the central government was given explicit limited powers, while the states retained all other powers.[20] This, the essence of states' rights, is plainly laid out in Article 2: "Each state retains its sovereignty, freedom, and independence, and every power, jurisdiction, and right, which is not by this Confederation expressly delegated to the United States, in Congress assembled."[21] This is why Jefferson Davis said: "It was not necessary in the Constitution to affirm the right of secession, because it was an attribute of sovereignty, and the states had reserved all which they had not delegated [to the central government]."[22]

TRUE OR FALSE: Secession was illegal when the Southern states began leaving the Union in December 1860.
ANSWER: False. Secession was perfectly legal at the time,[23] which is why then sitting President James Buchanan did nothing to stop the first seven states from seceding while he was still in office.[24]

MULTIPLE CHOICE: America's first attempt at secession occurred in
A. the West.
B. the East.
C. the South.
D. the North.

ANSWER: D. America's first true "rebellion" against the Union started in 1814 when a group of disgruntled Northern states began plans for secession and the formation of a "New England Confederacy."[25] The rebellion peaked at the famous Hartford Convention in 1815,[26] led by South-hating Massachusetts Senator Timothy Pickering, George Washington's former adjutant general,[27] and later President John Adams' secretary of state.[28]

Timothy Pickering.

TRUE OR FALSE: The American Union is meant to be "perpetual," which means that secession is illegal.
ANSWER: False. The word "perpetual" does not appear anywhere in

the U.S. Constitution.[29] Even if it did, the Founders never intended the Union itself to be perpetual. They intended the sovereignty of the individual states to be perpetual.[30] Preservation of this sovereignty, better known as states' rights, is precisely what the South fought for in 1861.[31]

QUESTION: How did the Founding Fathers view the states?

ANSWER: John Jay called the American colonies or states "distinct nations,"[32] Thomas Jefferson called them "little republics."[33] The Founding Generation as a whole referred to them as "nation-states."[34] Such terms reveal how our Founders envisioned the states: not as parts of a "perpetual" national conglomerate, but as small independent sovereign countries belonging to a voluntary union.[35]

John Jay.

MULTIPLE CHOICE: Which U.S. president supported secession before he took office but went against it afterward?

A. George Washington.

B. Ronald Reagan.

C. Abraham Lincoln.

D. Martin Van Buren.

ANSWER: C. Abraham Lincoln. On January 12, 1848, in a speech before the U.S. House of Representatives, our sixteenth chief executive declared: "Any people anywhere, being inclined and having the power, have the right to rise up, and shake off the existing government, and form a new one that suits them better. This is a most valuable, a most sacred right—a right which, we hope and believe, is to liberate the world. Nor is this right confined to cases in which the whole people of an existing government may choose to exercise it. Any portion of such people that can may revolutionize, and make their own of so much of the territory as they inhabit."[36]

When it was politically expedient to change his mind, Lincoln, of course, did just that. As U.S. president 13 years later, on July 4, 1861, in his "Message to Congress in Special Session," he called the new constitutionally formed Southern Confederacy an "illegal organization,"[37] and the constitutional right of secession an "ingenious sophism," an "insidious debauching of the public mind," and a "sugar-coated invention" of the South.[38] Those who challenged these views were labeled "traitors" and "rebels."[39]

James Madison.

TRUE OR FALSE: Secession is legal, it has always been legal, and it will always be legal.

ANSWER: True. The right of accession (*entering* a union) and the right of secession (*leaving* a union) are concomitant rights of sovereigns.[40] And as the Declaration of Independence, the Articles of Confederation, and the U.S. Constitution (the Ninth and Tenth Amendments of the Bill of Rights) overtly show,[41] the states were purposefully created by the Founders as autonomous self-governing bodies,[42] "free and independent states," as Thomas Jefferson called them,[43] with powers that are "numerous and indefinite," according to James Madison.[44]

QUESTION: Why did the Founding Fathers consider secession so important?

ANSWER: They viewed it as one of the few things that would guarantee personal liberty, which they considered the most valuable right of all.[45]

TRUE OR FALSE: Jefferson Davis led the Southern secession movement.

ANSWER: False. Then Mississippi Senator Davis could not have spearheaded the Southern secession movement, which officially began on December 20, 1860, for he waited until *after* his state seceded on January 9, 1861, before leaving the U.S. Senate.[46]

FILL IN THE BLANKS: Every county in every Southern state seceded except for various counties in the states of _____ and _____.

ANSWER: "Missouri and Kentucky." While only portions of these two states seceded, the Confederacy counted them as full states, forming the twelfth and thirteenth stars on the Confederate Battle Flag and on the National Confederate Flags.[47]

TRUE OR FALSE: The U.S. is a nation and secession is not legal under a national government.

ANSWER: True and false. It is true that nations do not normally permit secession. But the United States of America is not a nation[48]—for it was not intended to be a nation (an idea the Founders rejected)[49]—or even a *democracy* (the word does not appear in any of America's founding documents).[50] The U.S.A. was created as a "confederate republic,"[51] which is a different form of government than a nation or a democracy.[52]

The word *confederacy* describes our Union and is defined as a "friendly association" of states held together by "good faith," the "exchanges of equity and comity," and the concept of the separation of powers;[53] a compact of independent states, therefore, whose power, authority, and sovereignty rests on states' rights—one of which is secession. As for the word *republic*, it describes our form of government and is defined as a small, weak, decentralized government whose power resides in the people.[54] This makes America a confederate republic.[55]

It was for such reasons that our country was originally known as "the Confederacy" by the Founders, and her first Constitution was called the "Articles of Confederation." This is also why many Americans and foreigners once referred to our republic, the U.S.A., as "The Confederate States of America," and it is why, in 1861, the South called its new republic "The Confederate States of America."[56]

QUESTION: What is the primary reason secession was and is legal in the U.S.?

ANSWER: The Founders set up our confederate republic as a *voluntary* league of states.[57] It is this, the voluntary nature of our union, which gives each state the right to accede (enter) and secede (leave) at will.[58] Thus St. George Tucker noted that the states' "submission" to the operation of the government "is *voluntary*,"[59] while Alexis de Tocqueville asserted: "The [American] Union was formed by the *voluntary* agreement of States; and, in uniting together, they have not forfeited their nationality, nor have they been reduced to the condition of one and the same people. If one of the States chose to withdraw its name from the contract, it would be difficult to disprove its right of doing so; and the Federal Government would have no means of maintaining its claims directly either by force or by right."[60]

MULTIPLE CHOICE: The right of secession is

A. unconstitutional.

B. constitutional.

C. extraconstitutional.

ANSWER: B and C. Secession is constitutional because the Constitution contains no prohibition against it,[61] while the Ninth and Tenth Amendments (Bill of Rights) tacitly imply its legality.[62]

Secession is extraconstitutional (that is, outside the Constitution) because: 1) it is an unquestionable and innate right of sovereigns (as our states are);[63] 2) it is inferred as one of John Locke's indestructible God-given "natural rights";[64] 3) colonial constitutional scholars (one of them appointed a U.S. district attorney by Founding Father George Washington) declared it to be an integral "ingredient in the original composition of the general government";[65] and 4) it is an aspect of "the great Law of Nations, which govern all compacts between sovereigns."[66]

TWO

THE WAR

TRUE OR FALSE: The South started the Civil War when it fired the first shot at the Battle of Fort Sumter.

ANSWER: False. President Lincoln cunningly tricked the Confederacy into firing first through lying and deceit, the purpose being to put responsibility for inaugurating the conflict on the South.[67] The nefarious plot worked, and Lincoln later admitted as much;[68] as did his authorized biographers John G. Nicolay and John Hay, who said: "When the President determined on war, and with the purpose of making it appear that the South was the aggressor, he took measures . . ."[69] These "measures" were fraud, treachery, and dishonesty.

MULTIPLE CHOICE: The total number of Confederate soldiers killed during the War was

A. around 127,000.

B. at least 2 million.

C. about 56,000.

D. nearly 198,000.

ANSWER: B. The official number of Confederate dead is 329,000,[70] but this is a Northern calculation, and, as such, is meant to mislead and conceal. The actual figure is closer to 2 million dead, counting both white and black soldiers as well as civilians: 16 percent of Dixie's total white and black population (of 12 million). There are no records of how many Confederate Asian, Native-American, and Hispanic soldiers perished, but the number must be well into the tens of thousands.[71]

TRUE OR FALSE: The Civil War was given that name because it was a polite and civilized conflict.

ANSWER: False. The "civil" in civil war does not refer to civility, but to one of the term's other definitions, namely: "a war between opposing groups of citizens belonging to the same country."[72] As the North (the U.S.A.) and the South (the C.S.A.) were two separate confederate republics in April 1861, this term is clearly misleading, and is thus a false description of the war—which is precisely why the North invented it.[73]

Jefferson Davis.

TRUE OR FALSE: The Civil War was about slavery: the North fought to destroy it, the South fought to preserve it.

ANSWER: False. The highest officials on both sides, from Jefferson Davis and Robert E. Lee to Abraham Lincoln and Ulysses S. Grant, emphatically declared that the conflict was *not* over slavery. Indeed, as millions of Confederate and Union soldiers themselves stated, not one of them would have enlisted if it had been.[74]

QUESTION: If the Civil War was not about slavery, why was it fought?

ANSWER: It was a Victorian continuation of the age old battle between conservatism and liberalism—then as now, the South being essentially traditional and conservative, the North being essentially progressive and liberal.[75] This is, of course, what the major parties of that day tell us: in 1861 the Democrats (primarily Southerners) were Conservatives, the Republicans (primarily Northerners) were Liberals.[76]

MULTIPLE CHOICE: The South is still fighting the Civil War because

A. the War is not over.

B. Southerners are naturally pugnacious.

C. Southerners live in the past.

D. the South cannot accept that it lost.

ANSWER: A. The South does not tear down Union monuments, burn and ban the Union flag, or desecrate Union grave sites. But the North does all of these things and more to Confederate monuments, the

Confederate Flag, and Confederate grave sites. It is not the South who keeps the War going. It is the North. The South has little choice but to defend her history, honor, and heritage against the hate-filled intolerance and ignorance spread by Liberal South-haters—just as she had no choice when the North invaded her with 75,000 troops in April 1861. For this the South is charged with "still fighting the War."[77] So both sides remain engaged, for the ancient battle between conservatism and liberalism is endless. Thus Davis could say in 1881: "The contest is not over, the strife is not ended. It has only entered on a new and enlarged arena."[78]

TRUE OR FALSE: The Civil War was unnecessary.

ANSWER: True. There was never a more useless conflict in world history than the American Civil War. Why? Because slavery was not the issue and secession was legal. Thus there was no reason to fight. The Southern states had acted legally under both the Constitution and international law and only took up arms to *defend* hearth and home from the Yankee invaders, not to aggress against the North. Here we have the main reason the North rewrote the history of the War: to hide the truth that millions died for no other reason than the Left's desire to consolidate political power in Washington, D.C.[79]

TRUE OR FALSE: The South's cause was unrighteous, the North's was righteous. This is why the North won.

ANSWER: False. History has shown that the victor is not always the "good guy." One of many examples of this is the Vietnam War.[80] We must also consider the fact that the progressive North, under the reckless leadership of big government Liberal Abraham Lincoln, won primarily by ignoring the Constitution and international law. The conservative South, on the other hand, under the more cautious leadership of traditionalist Jefferson Davis, followed the Constitution, placing morals, ethics, and law above winning.[81]

FILL IN THE BLANKS: At its most basic level the Civil War was a contest over _____ _____.

ANSWER: "political principles." As noted, these were the principles of conservatism and liberalism. Though money, megalomania, greed, and ego also played a role, all were ultimately subservient to party politics.[82]

THREE

TOP POLITICAL

LEADERS

Thomas Jefferson.

QUESTION: Though political Conservative Thomas Jefferson died 35 years before the start of Lincoln's War, what major contribution did he unknowingly make to the founding of the Southern Confederacy? **ANSWER:** Writing in 1798 in response to the Liberals' unconstitutional "Alien and Sedition Laws," Jefferson formulated the "Kentucky Resolutions," which discussed and reemphasized such important constitutional ideas as the separation of powers and states' rights. In doing so the author of the Declaration of Independence validated the right of secession as a fully legal remedy for the South's grievances against the Union 62 years later.[83]

TRUE OR FALSE: If one combines personality, education, intelligence, honesty, compassion, authenticity, likeability, morality, and leadership qualities, Jefferson Davis was the greatest of the two Civil War presidents.
ANSWER: True. Davis was a West Point graduate, a Mexican War hero, a faithful husband, an outstanding father, an eminent Mississippi senator, a bold defender of the Southern Cause, a talented author, and a fearless and knowledgeable protector of the Constitution.

Also a guileless politician and a brave military man who was popular with his soldiers, Davis was an extraordinary leader of the Confederate republic during what was arguably America's most difficult period. A true Jeffersonian Conservative, he loved the U.S.A. and wholly supported the Constitution. In the eyes of the South these things alone make Davis not only a great man, but by far the greatest Civil War president.[84]

Jefferson Davis.

TRUE OR FALSE: Jefferson Davis founded the Southern secession movement.

ANSWER: False. Though being a constitutional scholar he understood and supported the right of secession, Davis was not the founder of the Southern secession movement, for its roots began in the late 1700s with the thoughts and writings of Thomas Jefferson and James Madison, and in particular, their "Kentucky and Virginia Resolutions," which they composed between the years 1798 and 1799.[85]

TRUE OR FALSE: Jefferson Davis was a traitor for siding with the Confederacy.

ANSWER: False. Secession was (and is) legal. Therefore seceding from the Union was not treason.[86] To the contrary, Davis was an American patriot for following state, constitutional, and natural law.[87]

TRUE OR FALSE: Jefferson Davis was not tried and executed after the War because the U.S. government could not find a prosecuting attorney to represent the Union.

ANSWER: True. Jefferson Davis, though arrested, charged, and imprisoned for "treason," was never given a complete trial; this despite the fact that he repeatedly requested one. Unfortunately for history, he was repeatedly turned down: the U.S. government had asked three different lawyers to try him, but all three refused, deeming the case unwinnable.[88] Why?

A full public trial would have allowed the South's brilliant legal minds, including Davis', to prove the legality of secession *and* expose what I call "The Great Yankee Coverup";[89] that is, the wholesale concealment of the many illegalities of Lincoln's War.[90]

TRUE OR FALSE: Jefferson Davis was a white racist who cared nothing for blacks.

ANSWER: False. While Davis, like nearly every other 19th-Century European-American, possessed the mild white racism that was part and parcel of Victorian society, it was nothing compared to the severe racism found among white Northerners at the time.

Consider President Lincoln, as just one example. While "Honest Abe" was blocking emancipation, black enlistment, and black civil rights, and working day and night on his colonization plan to deport all blacks out of the U.S.,[91] Davis was busy trying to figure out a way to end Southern slavery, enlist blacks, initiate black civil rights, and incorporate blacks into mainstream American society.[92]

During the War Davis and his wife Varina adopted a young black boy, Jim Limber, who they raised as their own in the Confederate White House.[93] The Davis family was widely known for the kind treatment they bestowed upon their black servants, who, in

Jefferson Davis and some of his family members, including his wife Varina (lower right).

customary Southern tradition, they viewed as part of their own family.[94] President Davis' first Confederate states marshal was a black man,[95] yet Lincoln never appointed a black man to any position, let alone U.S. states marshal, and unquestionably he would have never adopted a black child.[96]

After Lee's surrender, during the Davis family's escape southward, their coachman was a "faithful" free African-American.[97] Later, after the War, the one-time Southern leader and his wife sold their plantation, Brierfield, to a former slave.[98] Davis even spoke once of a time when he led a unit of "negroes against a lawless body of armed white men . . .,"[99] something we can be sure that white separatist Lincoln never did.[100]

FILL IN THE BLANKS: Due to his ardent love of the Constitution and traditional American values (Americanism), Conservative Jefferson Davis has long been known to Southerners as the _____ of _____.
ANSWER: "Patriot of Patriots."[101]

Alexander H. Stephens.

QUESTION: Why did Confederate Vice President Alexander H. Stephens say that the Confederacy was based on the "cornerstone" of slavery?
ANSWER: When he made his comment about slavery being the "cornerstone" of the C.S. Constitution, Stephens was merely repeating the words of a *Yankee* judge, Associate Justice of the U.S. Supreme Court Henry Baldwin of Connecticut, who, 28 years earlier, in 1833, had said: "Slavery is the corner-stone of the [U.S.] Constitution. The foundations of the Government are laid and rest on the rights of property in slaves, and the whole structure must fall by disturbing the corner-stone."[102] As Richard M. Johnston noted later in 1884, all Stephens did during his "Cornerstone Speech" was accurately point out the fact that "on the subject of slavery there was no essential change in the new [Southern Confederate] Constitution from the old [the U.S. Constitution]."[103]

MULTIPLE CHOICE: Stephens served as
A. vice president of the Confederate States of America.
B. a U.S. Georgia senator.
C. a U.S. Georgia state representative.
D. a U.S. Georgia governor.
ANSWER: All of the above. Stephens was one of the most ardent American patriots in our history, a true conservative nationalist who faithfully served two confederate republics in one governmental capacity or another almost nonstop from age 24 until his death at 71.[104]

Alexander H. Stephens.

TRUE OR FALSE: Stephens' supporters put his name forward as a Democratic (then Conservative) candidate for president of the United States (in 1859) and president of the Confederate States (in 1861).

ANSWER: True. Stephens turned down both offers, considering himself unqualified. (This was quite unlike Lincoln, who also believed he was "not fit to be president," but, much to the detriment of the country, accepted his party's nomination anyway.)[105]

In the 1860 election Stephens voted for Northern Democrat (conservative) Stephen A. Douglas, while during the formation of the C.S.A. he favored Robert A. Toombs for president (the position went to Jefferson Davis).[106]

TRUE OR FALSE: Widespread anti-Semitism in the South explains why Judah P. Benjamin was the only Jew in the Confederate government and military.

ANSWER: False. The South was not anti-Semitic and Benjamin himself proves it. Throughout his life the Conservative Southern Jew served in numerous U.S. government positions, including Louisiana senator and state legislator.[107] Faithfully following his state out of the Union in 1861, the Confederate government appointed Benjamin attorney general, secretary of war, and finally secretary of state under President Davis.[108] An admiring Southern public nicknamed Benjamin "the brains of the Confederacy,"[109] in part because, like every other major Southern leader, he promoted the idea of freeing and enlisting slaves in the Confederate military.[110]

Dislike of Jews in the South was essentially nonexistent. As further evidence we have the fact that some 12,000 Jewish-Americans courageously served in the Confederate military.[111] There were twenty Confederate Jewish staff officers alone,[112] men like Colonel Abraham Myers, the noted Jewish Confederate and West Point graduate after whom Fort Myers, Florida, was named.[113]

The real anti-Semitism was in the North, where Yankee leaders like Lincoln, Ulysses S. Grant, Benjamin F. Butler, and Elihu B. Washburne engaged in both the slander of Jewish-Americans and the infringement of their constitutional rights.[114]

TRUE OR FALSE: In January 1865, four months before the end of the War, Confederate Secretary of State Benjamin ordered Confederate commissioner Duncan F. Kenner to England to announce the Confederacy's commitment to full emancipation.
ANSWER: True.[115]

QUESTION: Why did Benjamin support the idea of emancipating then enlisting black slaves in the Confederate army and navy?
ANSWER: Not only was it the right thing to do (the South was, after all, the birthplace of the American abolition movement),[116] but countless thousands of Southern black servants supported the idea as well. Benjamin himself said: "We have 680,000 blacks capable of bearing arms, and who ought now to be in the field. Let us now say to every negro

Judah P. Benjamin.

who wishes to go into the ranks on condition of being free, 'go and fight—you are free.' My own negroes have been to me and said, 'Master, set us free and we'll fight for you.'"[117]

QUESTION: Why is Abraham Lincoln annually voted "America's best president"?
ANSWER: Because the truth about him has been carefully suppressed by his liberal, socialist, and communists followers. If the real Lincoln were known to the public today he would be voted "America's worst president."[118] And indeed, this is exactly what occurred during his tenure in the White House, for at the time the real Lincoln had not yet been concealed under a mountain of sentimental mythology, liberal tall tales, and obvious misrepresentations. This is why mid 19th-Century Americans considered him the most terrible president up to that time,[119] some even referring to him as "America's most hated president."[120]

MULTIPLE CHOICE: Lincoln was called "Honest Abe" due to his

Abraham Lincoln.

A. honesty.

B. stringent work ethic.

C. dishonesty.

D. integrity.

ANSWER: C. Contrary to Yankee myth, from his youth Lincoln had a reputation for dishonesty, mendaciousness, and perfidy. And this is how he earned the nickname "Honest Abe." It is, in other words, a reverse nickname, just as a tall man named John might be nicknamed "Little John." Here in the American South Lincoln is referred to more straightforwardly as "Dishonest Abe."[121]

TRUE OR FALSE: Lincoln was a Republican, and therefore a Conservative.

ANSWER: False. America's two main parties were reversed in 1860: at the time the Republicans were the Liberal party, the Democrats were the Conservative party, and they would remain this way until the infamous election of 1896—the year they switched platforms, becoming the parties we know today. Thus Lincoln was a big government Liberal (with socialistic leanings), Jefferson Davis was a small government Conservative (with libertarian leanings).[122]

MULTIPLE CHOICE: Traditional conservative Southerners still detest Lincoln, and always will, because, as his own words and actions prove, he was

A. a war criminal.

B. a big government Liberal.

C. the instigator of the IRS.

D. an anti-constitutionalist.

E. a South-hater.

F. a vulgarian.

G. an agnostic.

H. an anti-Christian.

I. a Bible-hater.

J. a white racist.

K. a white separatist.

L. a white supremacist.

M. a black colonizationist.

ANSWER: All of the above.[123]

TRUE OR FALSE: Lincoln saved the Union.

ANSWER: False. The Founding Fathers created the U.S.A. as a voluntary union[124] of "little republics"[125] or "nation-states,"[126] imbuing each one with the "assumed rights" of accession (entering) and secession (exiting).[127] By physically forcing the C.S. (Southern states) back into the U.S., Lincoln actually destroyed (or at least damaged) the "voluntary union of friendly states"[128] intended by the Founders.[129]

TRUE OR FALSE: Lincoln did not free any slaves.

ANSWER: True. The Emancipation Proclamation was worthless, toothless, and thus powerless, for it was issued in a constitutionally

The Emancipation Proclamation.

formed foreign country, the Confederate States of America, where the Union had no legal authority. According to the proclamation itself, it only freed slaves in sections of the South that had been captured by U.S. forces. Those still under Confederate control, and the thousands of slaves still held in the North, were, as Lincoln himself wrote in the document, "for the present left precisely as if this proclamation were not issued."[130] As a result, not a single Southern (or Northern) slave was legally freed. Authentic, lawful, and complete abolition across America would not come until the Thirteenth Amendment, issued in December 1865, eight months after Lincoln's death.[131]

QUESTION: What was Lincoln's plan for blacks after emancipation?
ANSWER: Lincoln did not have a post emancipation plan and showed little if any concern about the welfare of the millions of African-Americans he intended to set free. There would be no jobs, housing, healthcare, food, or clothing waiting for freedmen and women. All of this had been provided for free (in exchange for work, and in many cases without work) by the slaves' original owners. The "forty-acres-and-a-mule" offer turned out to be nothing but a cruel Yankee hoax, and since they were created merely as anti-South propagandizing agencies, the government-sponsored black Loyal Leagues and the Freedmen's Bureau were utterly useless, and actually made things much worse for both freed servants and their former owners.[132]

"Freed" slaves *after* the War under Yankee rule.

Fortunately for enslaved African-Americans, Lincoln's Emancipation Proclamation was illegal and therefore ineffectual. If it had been legal *and* effectual we can be sure that things would have turned out much worse for blacks than they actually did. When a concerned citizen asked the U.S. president what he planned do for newly freed slaves, he callously compared them to wild hogs, replying: "Let 'em root, pig, or perish!"

What I will call Lincoln's disastrous "Root, Pig, or Perish Emancipation Plan" actually went into effect after his death with the ratification of the Thirteenth Amendment. As a result, by 1867, just four years after the Emancipation Proclamation had been issued, some 25 percent of the South's African-American population had died from starvation, neglect, infanticide, corruption, and disease. Little wonder that Lincoln later opined that his Emancipation Proclamation had been "the greatest folly of my life."[133]

TRUE OR FALSE: Lincoln loved blacks, which is why he was America's greatest abolitionist.

ANSWER: False. Lincoln was neither a "friend of the black man" or our greatest abolitionist. In fact, for his entire adult life he espoused racist and anti-abolitionist views, some quite extreme.[134] He often said, for instance, that he hated the entire abolition movement[135] and that abolition was worse than slavery.[136] Once, when someone asked him

how he felt about having abolitionists in his party, he replied that it was not a problem, "as long as I'm not tarred with the abolitionist brush."[137]

Such sentiments explain why Lincoln stalled the Emancipation Proclamation for several years, was a leader in the racist Northern-founded "American Colonization Society," had slaves complete the construction of the White House, implemented severe racist military policies, used profits from Northern slavery to fund his War, often referred to blacks as "niggers" (both privately and publicly), said he was willing to allow slavery to continue in

Lincoln emancipating a slave: a Yankee fantasy that never occurred.

perpetuity if the seceded Southern states would return, pushed nonstop for the deportation of blacks, defended slave owners in court, and continually blocked black enlistment, black suffrage, and black citizenship.[138] He even supported the idea of corralling African-Americans in their all-black state,[139] saying publicly on July 17, 1858: "What I would most desire would be the separation of the white and black races."[140]

Lincoln's party, the Republican Party (which has no connection to today's Republican Party), was founded by Liberals and socialists in 1854 specifically to prevent the expansion of slavery, not abolish it.[141] This is why, in 1861, at the beginning of his presidency, Lincoln supported the Corwin Amendment, which would have allowed slavery to remain legal in Dixie if the Southern states agreed to rejoin the Union and pay their taxes.[142]

MULTIPLE CHOICE: Which American president publicly asked Congress to fund the deportation of blacks?
A. President John Tyler.
B. President Andrew Jackson.
C. President Abraham Lincoln.
D. President Franklin Pierce.
ANSWER: C. Abraham Lincoln.[143]

MULTIPLE CHOICE: What was the name of the speech or document in which Lincoln asked for congressional funding to ship blacks back to their own "native land"?
A. His First Inaugural Address.
B. The Morrill Act.
C. The Preliminary Emancipation Proclamation.
D. His Third Annual Message to Congress.
E. The Gettysburg Address.
F. The Wade-Davis Bill.
ANSWER: C. Lincoln issued his Preliminary Emancipation Proclamation on September 22, 1862. The importance of this document was later supplanted by the issuance of the Final Emancipation Proclamation on January 1, 1863. As a result the preliminary version is less well-known to the public.[144]

QUESTION: Why did Lincoln's appeal to Congress to fund black deportation not make it into his Final Emancipation Proclamation?
ANSWER: Lincoln's advisors told him that it might cause him to lose votes, particularly abolitionist votes, in his upcoming bid for reelection in 1864. So Lincoln removed it—but only reluctantly. Though the Final Emancipation Proclamation is the one best known to Americans, the Preliminary Emancipation Proclamation, with its call for black deportation, is clearly the version Lincoln preferred.[145]

In fact, to emphasize his support of black deportation and colonization, he issued another statement on the subject, this one in his Second Annual Message to Congress, which he gave on December 1, 1862. "I cannot make it better known than it already is," the president told the public that day, "that I strongly favor colonization."[146]

QUESTION: What high ranking member of the Lincoln administration later turned against the president, becoming one of his most vociferous detractors?

ANSWER: Lincoln's first vice president, Hannibal Hamlin. Other influential Republican (Liberal) Party members who became critics of Lincoln were William H. Seward, Edwin M. Stanton, Salmon P. Chase, Charles Sumner, and Lyman Trumbull.[147]

Hannibal Hamlin.

TRUE OR FALSE: U.S. Secretary of State William H. Seward was with Lincoln when the U.S. president told a group of Confederate diplomats that since the Emancipation Proclamation was nothing more than a temporary "war measure," it would cease to be active if and when the South gave up and returned to the Union, at which time the Southern people could resume practicing slavery if they so desired.

ANSWER: True.[148] Lincoln's statement was later attested to by all three of the Confederate commissioners present at the Hampton Roads Peace Conference held on February 3, 1865: Vice President Alexander H. Stephens, Senator Robert M. T. Hunter, and Assistant Secretary of War John A. Campbell.[149]

QUESTION: Why did Seward refer to the Civil War as the "irrepressible conflict"?

ANSWER: The statement was part of the Liberal North's propaganda efforts to portray the conflict as inevitable due to the "traitorous" secession of the Southern states. In truth, there was nothing "irrepressible" about the War. Not only had the South seceded legally,[150] but Confederate President Davis sent one envoy of peace commissioners after another to Washington before and throughout the conflict in an attempt to halt the bloodshed. Lincoln refused to meet with any of them. He only agreed to sit down with the Confederacy when he was sure that the North had won. As noted above, this took place in February 1865 (two months before the end of the War), at the notorious Hampton Roads Peace Conference in Virginia.[151]

MULTIPLE CHOICE: Union Secretary of State Seward supported the December 1860 Crittenden Resolutions because, providing the Southern states remained in the Union,

A. they would allow slavery to remain permanently untouched in the South.

B. they would permit the extension of slavery beyond the Missouri Compromise of 1850.

C. they would enable further strengthening of the Fugitive Slave Laws.

D. he was a white racist.

ANSWER: All of the above.[152]

William H. Seward.

TRUE OR FALSE: Though a Yankee, Seward of New York—who oversaw the purchase of Alaska from Russia in 1867—loved the South and the Southern people.

ANSWER: False. Seward was one of the thousands of Northern Liberals who invented and spread vicious falsehoods about Dixie, all part of the anti-South movement that was evident as far back as George Washington's presidency, and which continues unabated into the present day.[153]

QUESTION: How do we know that Seward was a white racist?

ANSWER: Because like Lincoln he made scores of racist statements, many of them in public. For example, on September 4, 1860, during a speech at Detroit, Michigan, Seward said: "The great fact is now fully realized that the African race here is a foreign and feeble element, like the Indians, incapable of assimilation . . . a pitiful exotic, unwisely and unnecessarily transplanted into our fields . . ."[154] This was only six months before Lincoln appointed him secretary of state in March 1861.

TRUE OR FALSE: Before he became part of the Lincoln administration Seward supported the idea of secession.

ANSWER: True. In 1844, for instance, Seward said: "This Union must be a voluntary one, and not compulsory. A Union upheld by force would be a despotism." Seward later adopted his boss' absurd policy, that secession was a "sugar-coated invention" of the South.[155]

FOUR

TOP MILITARY LEADERS

Robert E. Lee.

QUESTION: Why did Confederate General Robert E. Lee love slavery?
ANSWER: Lee did not love slavery, he hated it.[156] This is why he spent most of his adult life trying to figure out how to abolish it without hurting either slave owners or slaves themselves. His abolition plan included freeing and enlisting slaves in the Confederate military.[157]

TRUE OR FALSE: Lee was a slave owner.
ANSWER: False. Like many other Confederate officers, Lee did not own slaves. Though there were black servants in the Lee household, these belonged to the family of his wife Mary Ann Custis. Lee himself never personally purchased slaves, and, in accordance with his father-in-law's will, he emancipated all the Custis servants in 1862, three years before the U.S. officially abolished slavery in December 1865 (Thirteenth Amendment).[158]

TRUE OR FALSE: General Lee was a traitor to the U.S. for supporting secession.
ANSWER: False. To begin with, secession was legal in 1861, and still

is.[159] Second, Lee himself was against both secession and the idea of his home state leaving the Union. He only relented after Lincoln made his intentions clear at the Battle of Fort Sumter April 12, 1861. On April 17 Virginia seceded, and on April 20, following state, constitutional, and international law, Lee reluctantly resigned from the U.S. army, joining his fellow Virginians in the fight against Liberal Northern tyranny and oppression.[160]

MULTIPLE CHOICE: Lee would
A. not have surrendered if he had the chance to fight the War over.
B. still have surrendered if he had the chance to fight the War over.
C. would not have agreed to secession had he known the results of the War beforehand.
ANSWER: A. In 1870, shortly before his death and at the peak of Reconstruction, Lee told Fletcher Stockdale, the former Confederate governor of Texas: "Governor, if I had foreseen the use those people designed to make of their victory, there would have been no surrender at Appomattox Courthouse; no, sir, not by me. Had I foreseen these results of subjugation, I would have preferred to die at Appomattox with my brave men, my sword in this right hand."[161]

MULTIPLE CHOICE: Confederate General Nathan Bedford Forrest was considered by many, even Yankees, to be the greatest soldier
A. from Tennessee.
B. to fight in the Western Theater.
C. to fight in the Confederate army.
D. to fight in either the Confederate or the Union army.
ANSWER: D. He was later praised even by his most ardent former foes. One of these, Union General William T. Sherman, said of Forrest: he was "the most remarkable man the Civil War produced on either side."[162]

Nathan B. Forrest.

TRUE OR FALSE: Because Forrest was a slave owner he should be forever condemned, his monuments torn down, and his figure erased from our history books.

ANSWER: False. Judging our 19th-Century ancestors based on current ideas and mores (known as presentism) is always unfair and unethical, and leads to a host of problems, not the least of which is the creation of false history. If Forrest is to be denounced for being a slave owner, then so must many of our U.S. presidents, beginning with George Washington and Thomas Jefferson and ending with James K. Polk and Zachary Taylor. No one calls for the removal of their monuments simply because they had black servants under their roofs.

Those who make such absurd and bigoted comments ignore the facts that slavery was still legal in every state during Lincoln's War,[163] and that there were far more slave owning Union officers than slave owning Confederate officers,[164] Ulysses S. Grant being one of the most notable

General Forrest on the attack.

examples.[165] If Grant is a hero in the North, despite being both a slave owner and a black colonizationist, one who owned slaves before, during, and after the War,[166] then Forrest must be allowed to be a hero in the South despite being a slave owner as well. Anything else is but rank hypocrisy on the part of South-haters.[167]

TRUE OR FALSE: Forrest was one of the world's worst white racists, which is why he's despised by blacks to this day.

ANSWER: False. There are many thousands of blacks who admire, even love, Forrest—and for good reason. Those who do not are history-ignorant, for the distorted view expressed here, like nearly every other depiction of Forrest in our mainstream history books, is nothing but a fabrication of the Liberal anti-South movement, intentionally designed to demean our heroes and humiliate and punish the Conservative Christian South for daring to secede from the Union.[168]

The truth is that while Forrest exhibited the mild American racism endemic to that time period, it was nothing like South-haters claim. Evidence for this comes from his own words and actions.

For example, knowing and accepting that slavery was soon coming to an end, he willingly closed down his slave trading business and freed most of his slaves even before the War began.[169] After the start of the conflict he enlisted 45 of his servants in his cavalry, promising them their freedom (he emancipated them midway through),[170] then hand-picked seven of them to be his personal armed guards.[171] "These boys stayed with me, drove my teams, and better Confederates did not live," he proudly declared after the War.[172]

In 1875 Forrest was invited by an African-American sociopolitical group, the Independent Order of Pole Bearers (the forerunner of the NAACP), to speak at one of their meetings. During the address to his all-black audience he stated that he considered blacks his "brothers and sisters," adding: "I came here as a friend, and whenever I can serve any of you I will do so." Hardly the sentiments of a white racist.[173]

MULTIPLE CHOICE: What future Confederate general spent some of his childhood as a Huckleberry Finn-like runaway orphan on the Mississippi River?
A. John S. Mosby.
B. Albert S. Johnston.
C. Stonewall Jackson.
D. John Bell Hood.

Stonewall Jackson.

ANSWER: C. At age 12 Stonewall Jackson ran away from his uncle's home (where he had been sent to live after his parents died) with his older brother Warren. The pair traveled up and down the Big Muddy, cut wood for money, and lived in a "miserable" log cabin. Within a year the two returned home starving, sickly, and filthy—much smarter than when they left.[174]

TRUE OR FALSE: Stonewall Jackson was a slave owner.
ANSWER: False. Contrary to what South-hating Yankees and

uninformed scallywags teach, Jackson did not personally "own" slaves. It is true that the Census recorded black servants in his household, but this is not what makes one a slave owner. The fact is that he had purchased or taken them in at their own request. In other cases their original owners believed that Jackson could provide a better home for them than they could. It would be more accurate then to refer to "his" slaves as adoptees and Jackson himself as a reluctant adoptive guardian.[175]

QUESTION: How did General Jackson earn his reputation as a white racist?

ANSWER: Through the invention of lies designed to sully his honor, memory, and reputation. It must always be remembered that most of those Victorian Southern males who owned slaves (they made up only 4.8 percent of the total Southern population)[176] had the institution forced on them through the inheritance of their parents' slaves.[177]

As noted in the previous entry, Jackson was not a true slave owner, and neither was he a true racist. Like nearly every other Southerner, he detested slavery and supported abolition. His life matched his views.

Stonewall Jackson.

Finding the entire institution "troublesome," he desperately wanted his own servants to be independent freemen and women, which is why he set up a payment plan for them, allowing them to reimburse him for their original purchase and emancipate themselves as soon as possible.[178]

Another example: In the Fall of 1855 thirty-one year old Jackson opened up a Sunday school for some 100 African-Americans in Lexington, Virginia. He gave lessons and donated money to the small church, which he and his local white staff successfully maintained for many years. Later, after Jackson's death in 1863, grateful members of the General's African-American church donated money toward erecting a monument to him in the town of Lexington, Virginia.[179]

MULTIPLE CHOICE: What was Confederate General Patrick R. Cleburne most famous for?

A. His heroism on the battlefield.
B. His Irish birth.
C. The love his soldiers had for him.
D. His proposal to free all Southern slaves and enlist them in the Confederate armies.

ANSWER: All of the above.[180]

Patrick R. Cleburne.

QUESTION: What famous American folk hero fought as a Confederate guerrilla? **ANSWER:** Jesse James.[181]

TRUE OR FALSE: Yankee Union officer Ulysses S. Grant honorably and courageously earned his reputation as a war hero and general.
ANSWER: False. Real history, as opposed to the Liberals' fake history, records a different version. It is not widely known outside scholarly circles, but as the Battle of Fort Donelson (February 11-16, 1862) was unfolding, Grant's head was on the chopping block in Washington, D.C. Both his commander-in-chief, Major General Henry Wagner Halleck, and the general-in-chief of the U.S. army, General George Brinton McClellan, were chomping at the bit to arrest and imprison Grant.[182] Why?

Grant's superiors were running out of patience with him due to a number of acts of insubordination, including: disobeying orders, withdrawal from his command without leave, and traveling to Nashville without authorization.[183] Of this situation Grant himself later admitted that Halleck had "ordered that I should be relieved from duty and that an investigation should be made into any charges against me. He even authorized my arrest. Thus in less than two weeks after the victory at Donelson, the two leading generals in the army were in correspondence as to what disposition should be made of me, and in less than three weeks I was virtually in arrest and without a command."[184]

Relieved of his command by Halleck, but then restored on March 13, 1862, Grant was only a hair's breath away from becoming a felon.[185] What saved him from certain arrest, court martial, and prison?

It was the unnecessary Confederate surrender at Fort Donelson, which handed the Union a complimentary victory. With this one stroke of fortune, Grant, though he had not earned it, became an instant hero in the eyes of the Northern populace, which simultaneously guaranteed him an eternal place in the military hall of fame while lifting the official accusations against him. All of this, in turn, transformed Grant into a symbol of the Union's victory, quite naturally leading to his eventual election to president of the U.S. in 1868. As President of the nation's second most corrupt

Ulysses S. Grant.

administration (after Lincoln), Grant, a Liberal (then a Republican), continued to wound and humiliate the South, supporting and maintaining Reconstruction with brute military force until he left office in 1877.[186]

MULTIPLE CHOICE: Grant said he would rather join the Confederacy than fight for
A. the Constitution.
B. abolition.
C. secession.
D. the Republican Party.
ANSWER: B. During the conflict General Grant made this revealing comment: "The sole object of this war is to restore the union. Should I be convinced it has any other object, or that the government designs using its soldiers to execute the wishes of the Abolitionists, I pledge to you my honor as a man and a soldier, I would resign my commission and carry my sword to the other side."[187]

QUESTION: Why was Grant against abolition?
ANSWER: Because he was a slave owner and a white racist; one who evinced no sympathy for the situation of American blacks, never discussed the Underground Railroad, and did not show any personal interest in his colored chattel.[188]

Upon his marriage to Julia Boggs Dent in 1848, Grant inherited a small army of 30 black Maryland slaves that belonged to her family. Later, in 1858, he was known to still own "three or four slaves, given to his wife by her father," Colonel Frederick Dent. Technically, none of this made him a slave owner. However, he went on to lease several additional slaves, and personally purchased at least one (a 35 year old black man named William Jones)—which *did* make him an official slave owner. Revealingly, he never once showed a desire to free either his own slaves or Julia's. Instead, like his wife, and most other Northerners at the time, Grant assumed that the white race was superior to non-white races, and that this was simply the natural order of things.[189]

On the eve of Lincoln's War in early 1861, Grant grew increasingly excited over the possibility that a conflict with the South would greatly depreciate black labor, then, he happily exclaimed, "the nigger will never disturb this country again."[190] In an 1862 letter to his father Jesse Root Grant, General Grant wrote: "I have no hobby of my own with regard to the negro, either to effect his freedom or to continue his bondage."[191]

TRUE OR FALSE: Grant may have been a slave owner but he freed his slaves as soon as he could.
ANSWER: False. Grant's apathy for the black man continued throughout Lincoln's War. In 1863 he wrote: "I never was an abolitionist, not even what could be called anti-slavery." Even after the issuance of Lincoln's Emancipation Proclamation Grant maintained the same sentiment, noting sourly that white Americans were now still "just as free to avoid the social intimacy with the blacks as ever they were."[192]

Ulysses S. Grant.

Since Lincoln's bogus and illicit Emancipation Proclamation on January 1, 1863, did not liberate slaves in the North (or anywhere else, for that matter),[193] Grant was permitted to keep his black chattel—which is precisely what he did. In fact, he did not free them until he was forced to by the passage of the Thirteenth Amendment on December 6, 1865, which occurred eight months *after* Lincoln's death and the War had ended.[194]

MULTIPLE CHOICE: Union General William T. Sherman, who created so much unnecessary carnage across Dixie, specialized in burning down Southern homes and turning entire Confederate families into starving wandering refugees. What was the nickname given to the countless house ruins he left behind?

A. Sherman's Sentinels.

B. Sherman's Guards.

C. Sherman's Lookouts.

William T. Sherman.   D. Sherman's Scouts.

ANSWER: A. The name derived from the fact that after Sherman passed through a Southern town all that was left of the homes were smouldering chimneys.[195]

MULTIPLE CHOICE: Sherman was also adept at destroying Southern railroads. What nickname was given to the useless piles of rail he left behind?

A. Sherman's Knots.

B. Sherman's Snarls.

C. Sherman's Neckties.

D. Sherman's Tangles.

ANSWER: C. The name came from the fact that Sherman left the track twisted into various bow-like shapes.[196]

TRUE OR FALSE: Sherman well deserved his reputation in the South as a heartless, racist, violent South-hating devil.

ANSWER: True. And here are just a few of the reasons. Sherman and his men were known to laugh when the

"Sherman's Sentinels."

Southern women whose homes they were destroying would "cry aloud for mercy."[197] Admitting that he pilfered some $20 million from Southern banks and citizens, and bragging that he had destroyed $100 million worth of private property, Sherman then declared that the enormous number of Southerners he and his men had killed was "a beautiful sight," for the quicker more of them died, the sooner the War would end.[198]

At Atlanta, Georgia, he illegally forced the deportation of thousands of citizens, then attempted to bomb the town into gravel. Razing most of the private homes there, by the time the ruthless Yankee general departed, 90 percent of the city was literally nonexistent. His troops robbed girls and women of their trinkets, and even vandalized Southern cemeteries, digging up corpses for their jewelry.[199] So lightly did Sherman and his men take such crimes upon the Southern citizenry that they humorously referred to it as "treasure-seeking," enjoyable "excitements of the march."[200]

Beloved family pets, mainly dogs and cats, were shot on the spot, along with any other type of animal, such as horses, pigs, hogs, geese, and cattle, that could not be carried off.[201] In one typical case a Union soldier saw some Southern children playing with a frisky young greyhound. Walking over to the startled children, the insolent bluecoat grabbed the puppy and cruelly pummeled its brains out in front of them.[202]

Those Atlantans who were not beaten, arrested, or killed, fled into the mountains. Those civilians unlucky enough to be left behind faced a demonic force of unparalleled evil. Writes Stonebraker: "At one place Sherman took four hundred factory girls and sent them north of the Ohio River, away from home and friends. Such things are inhuman, and one's blood is made to boil to even relate

William T. Sherman.

them. All the white inhabitants were made to leave the city without regard to age or condition. All who would not take Lincoln's oath were sent South to famish. Such a stream of men, women and children with their all in their hands, could be seen wending their way from the desolated city. [Confederate General John Bell] Hood retorted against this cruelty, but Sherman said, 'War is cruelty! This year we will take your property, and next year your lives!'"[203]

TRUE OR FALSE: Sherman had nothing personal against Southerners. He was merely being a good soldier, one whose adroit leadership helped win the War for the Union.

ANSWER: False. Sherman went far beyond soldiering into the realm of overt criminality. On October 29, 1864, at Rome, Georgia, for instance, he sent out an order to a subordinate officer that read: "Cannot you send over about Fairmount and Adairsville, burn ten or twelve houses of known secessionists, kill a few at random, and let them know that it will be repeated every time a train is fired on from Resaca to Kingston?"[204] All three of the commands in Sherman's order were illegal, immoral, unchristian, and heinous, as well as gross violations of both national law and the Geneva Conventions.[205]

As far as what he thought of Southerners, here is what Sherman said about them in a June 21, 1864, dispatch to Edwin M. Stanton, Lincoln's secretary of war: "But one thing is certain, there is a class of people, men, women, and children, who must be killed or banished before you can hope for peace and order . . ."[206]

QUESTION: Where is the proof that Sherman was a racist?

ANSWER: We will let "Uncle Billy," as his men called him, speak for himself. On one occasion, for example, he said: "A nigger as such is a most excellent fellow, but he is not fit to marry, associate, or vote with me or mine."[207] Many more such comments could be given.

Benjamin F. Butler.

MULTIPLE CHOICE: Union General Benjamin F. Butler was most infamous for what policy?

A. His Children Order.

B. His Negro Order.

C. His Woman Order.

D. His Man Order.

ANSWER: C. After Butler subdued New Orleans in April 1862, he issued his notorious "Woman Order." According to the arrogant decree, Southern females who showed the slightest hint of "contempt" toward Yankee soldiers (including even "disrespectful" facial expressions) were to be treated as "whores," subject to arrest and imprisonment.[208]

William B. Mumford.

TRUE OR FALSE: Yankee officer Butler loved the South and did everything he could to protect Confederate citizens during the War.

ANSWER: False. It would be more accurate to say that he did everything in his power to destroy Dixie and harass and injure everyday Southern people. One example in particular aptly reveals the true character of the man.

In the Spring of 1862 William B. Mumford, a Confederate citizen and an inhabitant of New Orleans, pulled down a U.S. flag that Butler's troops had run up over the city's mint. Though the town had not been legally occupied by U.S. troops yet, though Mumford was a non-combatant with no criminal record, and though Mumford's wife and family pled for his life, Butler had the 42 year old strung up and hanged "in cold blood." For this illegal act of unwarranted cruelty President Davis issued a proclamation calling Butler a "felon deserving of capital punishment," who hence became known in the South by the well-deserved nickname "the Beast."[209]

MULTIPLE CHOICE: What made Union General John C. Frémont unique among all other officers in the U.S. military?

A. He was nicknamed the "Pathfinder" for his exploits as a noted American explorer.

B. Before the War he had been court-martialed for mutiny.

C. As a socialist Frémont had among the highest number of Lincoln's socialist, radical, and revolutionary followers in his army.

John C. Frémont.

D. After Lincoln reenslaved the slaves Frémont had emancipated in his military district (in Missouri), the Union president relieved Frémont of his command.

E. He referred to Lincoln as a "well-meaning baboon" and the "original gorilla."

F. In 1856 Frémont became the first presidential candidate of the new Republican Party (founded in 1854), the major Liberal party of that era (and in no way connected to the Republican Party of today).

G. His wife (and the author's cousin) was Virginia-born Jessie Ann Benton, daughter of famed Missouri Senator Thomas Hart Benton, a Democrat (then a Conservative) who voted against him in 1856.

ANSWER: All of the above.[210]

QUESTION: What Yankee officer, famous for commanding the first all-black Union troop, held that the main purpose of emancipation was not to establish black civil rights but to allow black enlistment?

ANSWER: Colonel Thomas Wentworth Higginson.[211]

Thomas W. Higginson.

FILL IN THE BLANKS: Higginson was a member of the _____ _____, a clandestine group that helped finance arch South-hater and Yankee madman John Brown.

ANSWER: "Secret Six." The names of the other five individuals were Gerrit Smith, Theodore Parker, Samuel Gridley Howe, George L. Stearns, and Franklin B. Sanborn. It was the money from these six Northerners that helped fund Brown's insane murder spree across the country, which in turn fanned the flames that led to the War for Southern Independence. Not the flames of the South's small proslavery movement, as Yankee myth teaches, but the flames of the South's massive states' rights movement.[212]

FIVE
MEMORABLE
CIVILIANS

QUESTION: Mary Chesnut of South Carolina was famous for what achievement?

ANSWER: Mary kept an enormous diary during Lincoln's War that exposes many of the lies of the anti-South movement. For example, the noted diarist and her husband James Chesnut Jr., Jefferson Davis' aide-de-camp, were slave owners who despised slavery, yearned for abolition, and treated their servants like members of their own family. You would never know any of this from reading mainstream history books, however. Mary showed that such attitudes and behaviors were typical across the white South, not atypical as Liberal historians would like you to believe.[213]

Belle Boyd.

MULTIPLE CHOICE: Which of the following is true of Belle Boyd of West Virginia?

A. She was an actress.

B. She was a mother.

C. She was a Confederate spy.

D. She was an adventurer.

ANSWER: All of the above. Miss Belle's real life story reads like a novel: at the start of Lincoln's War she killed a Union soldier who insulted her mother; she worked as a courier-spy for such Confederate generals as Stonewall Jackson and P. G. T. Beauregard; she was exiled once, arrested six times (once at sea), and imprisoned three times; she later married one of the Yankee officers who arrested her; she wrote a book called *Belle Boyd, In Camp and Prison*; she toured the U.S., lecturing on her wartime exploits; she became a stage actress; she married several more times and bore at least five children; in 1900, while speaking in Wisconsin, the 56 year old "Siren of the Shenandoah" died of a heart attack and was buried in Spring Grove Cemetery, Wisconsin Dells.[214]

Walt Whitman.

QUESTION: What did the "all-American poet" Walt Whitman have in common with his idol Abraham Lincoln?

ANSWER: Certainly one of the more striking similarities was their white racism: though they never met personally, Whitman and Lincoln evinced an open disdain for African-Americans, whom they both often referred to as "niggers."[215] Whitman, whose grandfather had owned slaves on Long Island, New York, once acknowledged his true feelings toward blacks when he said: "I don't care for the niggers."[216]

Lincoln, a white apartheid proponent and an ardent lifelong supporter of black deportation,[217] once famously declared that he had never intended to "set the niggers and white people to marry together."[218]

QUESTION: What was Rose O'Neill Greenhow noted for?

ANSWER: Greenhow of Montgomery County, Maryland, will live forever in the memories of traditional Southerners as a true Confederate heroine, one who risked her life spying for the Confederate States. Captured, she

Rose O. Greenhow and daughter.

spent time in a Northern prison, after which she was deported to the South. Returning from a trip to England in 1864, her ship ran aground off North Carolina. Tragically, the small boat she attempted to take ashore sank in the waves and she drowned. She recorded her memoirs in the delightfully pro-South book, *My Imprisonment and the First Year of Abolition Rule at Washington.*[219]

QUESTION: Who donated the land for the only privately owned Confederate cemetery in the U.S.?

ANSWER: John W. McGavock of Franklin, Tennessee. In April 1866 he gave two acres of his property on Carnton Plantation for the reburial of the remains of nearly 2,000 Confederate soldiers who had perished earlier on November 30, 1864, at the Battle of Franklin (II).[220] Shortly after the battle they had been hurriedly buried in makeshift graves without proper stone markers. The committee set up to

John W. McGavock.

fund what would come to be called the "McGavock Confederate Cemetery,"[221] included McGavock's son-in-law Confederate Captain George L. Cowan,[222] who served in General Nathan Bedford Forrest's famous cavalry Escort during the War.[223]

QUESTION: Why is William B. Mumford of New Orleans, Louisiana, considered a hero in the South?

ANSWER: Mumford tore down the U.S. Flag from the top of the city's mint, which had been hoisted there illegally by Union troops under General Benjamin F. "the Beast" Butler. Faithful to the Confederacy and the Constitution to the end, Mumford made the ultimate sacrifice. His unlawful execution by Butler made him an eternal martyr for the Southern Cause.[224]

QUESTION: Why does the name Augustin Metoyer stand out in the annals of American history?

ANSWER: Augustin was the head of one of the thousands of wealthy African-American slave-owning families, in this case from New Orleans.

The black anti-abolitionist clan owned some 400 black slaves, making them among the wealthiest people in the U.S., South and North, then and now.[225]

Harriet B. Stowe.

TRUE OR FALSE: Yankee author Harriet Beecher Stowe was an expert on slavery, which is why her book *Uncle Tom's Cabin* was so successful.

ANSWER: False. Stowe was a novelist and her book was a work of fiction, based not on fact, but on the emotional opinions of South-hating Northern abolitionists. She had never been to the South and knew nothing about Southern slavery—or even Northern slavery for that matter. Her book, roundly criticized by educated people both South and North, was only a commercial success because she told her Liberal readers what they wanted to hear; namely that Southern slavery was a "sin" and Southern slave owners were "criminals."[226] Of course, like other Yankee critics of Southern slavery, Stowe neglected to mention that American slavery got its start in the North, and that the American abolition movement first arose in the South.[227]

QUESTION: What notoriously racist organization was supported not only by Harriet Beecher Stowe, but also by President Abraham Lincoln, Horace Greeley (owner of the New York *Tribune*), William Lloyd Garrison (founder of *The Liberator*), Jared Sparks (president of Harvard University), Henry Rutgers (after whom Rutgers University is named), and Edward Everett (after whom the city of Everett, Massachusetts, is named), as well as thousands of other well-known Yankees?

ANSWER: The American Colonization Society, a white Yankee organization dedicated to "making America white from coast to coast" through the deportation of African-Americans.[228]

QUESTION: Who was Charles A. Dana and why is he so important to any study of the American Civil War?

ANSWER: Dana was a socialist from New Hampshire who was appointed to serve as President Lincoln's assistant secretary of war. Why would Dana, also the managing editor of socialist Horace Greeley's New York *Tribune*[229] and a personal friend of the founder of modern communism Karl Marx,[230] be asked to work in the Republican Party?[231] For the same reason thousands of other progressives and revolutionaries ended up serving various posts in the Union government and military.

Charles A. Dana.

Lincoln's Republican Party, founded in 1854, was the Left-wing party of that day, founded by Liberals and socialists who wanted to see a big government Liberal—either socialist Frémont or progressive Lincoln—in the White House.[232] Dana's presence in the Lincoln administration, along with thousands of other radicals filling both government and military positions, reveals the true political nature of the president and his left-leaning constituency.[233]

TRUE OR FALSE: Abolitionist John Brown's 1859 movement to start black riots in the South, by forming an army of slaves to kill whites and take over and destroy Dixie, was perfectly timed.

ANSWER: False. Brown's goal to start a "Civil War" over slavery was doomed from the start by not only bad timing, but by ignorance and bigotry.

In 1859 slavery was not the central issue in either the South or the North. It was only an issue among radical Yankee Liberals and a few extreme Southern progressives. The main concern across America that year was the upcoming 1860 presidential election. Who would end up in the White House, a big government Liberal or a small government Conservative? The Southern states were hinging their decision on whether to secede or not based on the outcome, making it, arguably, the most momentous election in American history.[234]

But there was another reason Brown's abolitionary war movement came at the wrong time, and therefore had no chance of success. It had been widely known for years that slavery was well on its way toward "ultimate extinction," as even Lincoln admitted.[235] Southerners (the ones responsible for launching the American abolition movement centuries earlier)[236] were just as aware of this fact as Northerners. In February 1861, for example, two months before the start of the War, Jefferson Davis told his wife Varina that no matter who won the coming conflict, slavery would be abolished.[237]

Thus, meddling left-wing Yankees like Brown stood little chance of starting up a revolution over the peculiar institution, particularly in the South in 1859.[238]

TRUE OR FALSE: Brown's raid on Harpers Ferry and his noble efforts to end slavery in the South were widely supported by the North.
ANSWER: False. Literally no one responded to Brown's pleas to join

John Brown.

his small band of psychopathic abolitionists (which was made up primarily of family members and friends). As for overall public support, it was noticeably absent—except for a handful of South-hating New England socialists like Henry David Thoreau, Ralph Waldo Emerson, and Theodore Parker.[239] Lincoln himself repudiated Brown's insane plot,[240] while famed black abolitionist Frederick Douglass considered it a suicide mission.[241]

Proof that Brown's idea to destroy slavery through violence was wholly misguided was the fact that there was not a single slave revolt in the South just before[242] or during Lincoln's War.[243] And neither was there a great migration of African-Americans out of the South after Lincoln's Emancipation Proclamation. In fact, over 95 percent of Southern blacks remained in Dixie, more evidence that there was no such thing as the "racist Old South."[244]

None of this should surprise us. The coming war between North and South would not be about slavery, as all the highest leaders on both sides declared before, during, and after the conflict.[245] Thus the Radical Liberals' antebellum abolition movement (which depended solely on physical force) was an unpopular highly criticized failure and Brown swung on the gallows for nought.[246]

TRUE OR FALSE: John Brown loved black people and was sincerely sympathetic to the cause of abolition.

ANSWER: False. If Brown had truly wanted to help enslaved African-Americans, the last thing he should have done is try to initiate a slave war in the South. Not only did his illegal, immoral, and sanguinary plan fail for lack of support, it actually backfired, for it merely strengthened the resolve of the Southern states to handle abolition in their own time and way.[247]

Brown's admiration of blacks is also suspect. Victorian Liberals (like Liberals today) viewed minorities primarily as a tool for accruing political power and enlarging the federal government.[248] Proof of his real attitude toward African-Americans comes from the fact that his first victim during his Harpers Ferry Raid was not a white slave owner, but rather a free non-slave owning black man named Heyward Shepherd. Shepherd refused to join Brown's mob of madmen, and so the Connecticut lunatic murdered him in cold blood.[249]

TRUE OR FALSE: Frederick Douglass disliked Abraham Lincoln due to his white racism, and was known to denounce the deceased president in public.

ANSWER: True. Evidence for Douglass' feelings toward Lincoln is plentiful. For example, he refused to vote for Lincoln in the 1860 election,[250] then later complained when the Liberal president would not allow blacks to fight as Union soldiers during the first half of the War (in contrast the Confederacy had

Frederick Douglass.

been allowing blacks to fight in its armies since day one).[251]

When asked what he thought of Lincoln's attitude toward African-Americans, Douglass replied: "The genuine spark of humanity is missing in it. It expresses merely the desire to get rid of them . . ."[252] How true, for Lincoln had been a lifelong member of the American Colonization Society,[253] a white racist group whose chief aim, like the Liberal party of that day (the Republicans of 1854),[254] was to "make the U.S. as white as New England"[255] by shipping African-Americans to foreign countries.[256]

During a speech at the "Unveiling of the Freedman's Monument in Memory of Abraham Lincoln" in Washington, D.C. on April 14, 1876, Douglass sourly described our sixteenth chief executive this way: "In his interests, in his associations, in his habits of thought, and in his prejudices, he was a white man. He was preeminently the white man's President, entirely devoted to the welfare of white men."[257]

Ralph W. Emerson.

TRUE OR FALSE: Famed American writer Ralph Waldo Emerson was a Yankee socialist who loathed Southerners.
ANSWER: True. Like Nathaniel Hawthorne, Theodore Parker, George Ripley, William Henry Channing, Margaret Fuller, Henry David Thoreau, Amos Bronson Alcott, and thousands of other Northerners, Emerson was a political progressive with socialist views.[258]

Another trait he shared with his left-wing friends was a hearty dislike of the Southern people, whom he considered stupid, conceited, and nearly as "uncivilized as Indians." The average Southerner was, he wrote, a "spoiled child, with graceful manners, excellent self-command, very good to be spoiled more, but good for nothing else,—a mere parader. . . he is dumb and unhappy, like an Indian in a church."[259]

MULTIPLE CHOICE: Which South-hating radical abolitionist did New England socialist Henry David Thoreau compare to Jesus?
A. Wendell Phillips.

B. Thaddeus Stevens.
C. John Brown.
D. William Lloyd Garrison.

ANSWER: C. Thoreau idolized arch criminal Brown, even likening him to the crucified Christ.[260] But were there really any similarities? Unlike Brown, Jesus never married and had no children. Jesus never spoke out against slavery nor did He hate anyone, as Brown did. Jesus did not divide humanity according to their race or judge others by their skin color, as Brown did. Jesus was not a deranged killer and He was not executed because He was found guilty of the

Henry D. Thoreau.

crimes of treason, conspiracy, and first-degree murder, as Brown was.[261] Despite these facts, to this day uneducated Liberals and misinformed Conservatives continue to depict the racist psychopath from New England as an example of the "ideal Christian."

William L. Garrison.

TRUE OR FALSE: Lincoln's personal friend and biographer John Hay described the president as "tyrannous" and admitted that he had purposely tricked the South into firing the first shot of the War at Fort Sumter.
ANSWER: True.[262]

QUESTION: Which famous New England abolitionist was set upon and dragged through the streets of Boston, Massachusetts, by an angry anti-abolitionist Yankee lynch mob in 1835, barely escaping with his life?
ANSWER: William Lloyd Garrison, more proof that the coming Civil War would not be over slavery.[263]

Horace Greeley.

MULTIPLE CHOICE: New York newspaperman and abolitionist Horace Greeley

A. was a socialist.

B. was a friend of Karl Marx (who contributed articles to his paper, the New York *Tribune*).

C. acknowledged the legal right of secession and urged the Union to let the Southern states secede in peace.

D. hired fellow radical socialists, like Charles A. Dana (Lincoln's assistant secretary of war), to work for his newspaper.

E. was told by Lincoln that if the Union could be saved without freeing a single slave he would do it.

F. was a supporter of black deportation and the American Colonization Society.

G. admitted that the South had enlisted blacks as real armed soldiers long before the North did.

H. was known for his eccentric attire.

I. was disliked by most Northerners because he was pro-abolition and anti-slavery.

J. signed the bail bond for imprisoned Confederate President Jefferson Davis after the War, donating $25,000 (the equivalent of about $413,000 in today's currency) to help pay for it.

K. ran for president in 1872 (against Ulysses S. Grant) as the candidate of the Liberal Republican Party, founded by Lincolnian socialist Carl Schurz, and which was a reformist spinoff of the regular Republican Party (the main Liberal party of that time period).

L. died near the end of November 1872, even before the final votes of the election had been cast.

ANSWER: All of the above.[264]

QUESTION: Which one of Lincoln's pre-White House law partners described the president as a church-hating agnostic who "did not believe that Jesus was God, nor the Son of God," asserting that Lincoln once wrote an anti-Christian book in which he called Jesus a bastard and biblical miracles unscientific? **ANSWER:** William H. Herndon, one of the president's colleagues and biographers. "Mr. Lincoln told me a thousand times," wrote Herndon, "that he did not believe the Bible was the revelation of God."[265]

Karl Marx.

MULTIPLE CHOICE: Jim Limber is the name of a young black boy who
A. Abraham Lincoln adopted during the War.
B. Frederick Douglass adopted during the War.
C. Harriet Beecher Stowe adopted during the War.
D. Jefferson Davis adopted during the War.
ANSWER: D.[266] During Davis' capture in Georgia in May 1865, the U.S. government cruelly tore little Jim from the arms of his adoptive family, emotionally devastating both the child and the president and his wife Varina. Jim disappeared without a trace, and the Davis' were never able to discover what happened to him.[267]

QUESTION: What foreign radical socialist idolized Lincoln and wrote him a letter in 1861 congratulating the big government Liberal on his presidential win?
ANSWER: The founder of modern communism, Russian revolutionary Karl Marx.[268]

Adolf Hitler.

QUESTION: What modern national socialist admired Lincoln and his attempt to stamp out states' rights in the American South?
ANSWER: The leader of the Nazi Party, German fascist Adolf Hitler, who respectfully referenced Lincoln in his famous autobiography *Mein Kampf*.[269] Though they represented two different aspects of socialism,[270] both Lincoln and Hitler were left-wingers, with dozens of personal traits, political ideas, and governmental policies in common.[271]

QUESTION: Who was Z. B. Mayo, and why is he important to American history?

Edmund Ruffin.

ANSWER: Mayo was a white newspaper editor who promoted the idea of putting African-Americans in their own all-black state. The reason he is of interest is that his plan was backed by Illinois Liberal Abraham Lincoln. On September 15, 1858, at one of his debates with Illinois Conservative Stephen A. Douglas, Lincoln read the following quote from Mayo: "Our opinion is that it would be best for all concerned to have the colored population in a State by themselves." Lincoln himself then said: "In this I agree with him."[272] A little over two years later he would be elected America's sixteenth president.

TRUE OR FALSE: Edmund Ruffin of Virginia typified the general attitude that Southerners had toward Northerners in the mid 19th Century.

ANSWER: True. After the War, Ruffin, a strong states' activist, committed suicide rather than live under Yankee rule. Though few Southerners actually took this extreme measure, after decades of abuse by Yankee Liberals the vast majority held the same negative view of their Northern neighbors as Ruffin did. In fact, many hundreds of Confederate families moved out of the U.S. to avoid Yankee "reconstruction"; some to South America,[273] many as far away as Europe.[274]

QUESTION: What Massachusetts abolitionist made public the fact that Lincoln had used profits from the Yankee slave trade to fund the Civil War?

ANSWER: Lysander Spooner. This historical truth has long been known in the South but is still ignored or suppressed in the North.[275]

Lysander Spooner.

Thaddeus Stevens.

QUESTION: What radical South-hating socialist called for the execution of Southern slave owners, the illegal seizure of their plantations, and the redistribution of their property to other progressives?
ANSWER: Thaddeus Stevens of Massachusetts, surely the most malevolent enemy the South had in the 19th Century.[276] Tragically, Lincoln adopted several of these heinous policies during his War.[277]

TRUE OR FALSE: After the War all Yankees supported the idea of Northernizing the South.
ANSWER: False. Many thousands of Yankees opposed the dastardly plan, known as "Reconstruction" in the North. In 1883 one of them, Albion W. Tourgee of Ohio, wrote an entire book on the subject, the theme which he encapsulated in the following passages: "The North and the South are simply convenient names for two distinct, hostile, and irreconcilable ideas,—two civilizations they are sometimes called, especially at the South. . . . These two must always be in conflict until the one prevails, and the other falls. To uproot the one, and plant the other in its stead, is not the work of a moment or a day. That was our mistake. We [Yankees] tried to superimpose the civilization, the idea of the North, upon the South at a moment's warning. We presumed, that, by the suppression of rebellion, the Southern white man had become identical with the Caucasian of the North in thought and sentiment; and that the slave, by emancipation, had become a saint and a Solomon at once. So we tried to build up communities there which should be identical in thought, sentiment, growth, and development, with those of the North. It was *a fool's errand*."[278]

TRUE OR FALSE: Sojourner Truth, an African-American women's and civil rights advocate, was one of Lincoln's best friends.
ANSWER: False. The idea that Lincoln had so-called "black friends" is just another preposterous myth, fabricated after his death by his devotees to conceal the president's lifelong white racism. Proof is extensive.

On February 25, 1862, for example, a year into Lincoln's first term,

Miss Truth was denied admission to the White House on account of her skin color. (Revealingly, Lincoln either created this rule or allowed an earlier one to remain on the books.) On other occasions she was able to make her way inside, but, according to her own testimony, she was seldom made to feel welcome, had to wait longer than whites, and was never received with any "reverence." An eyewitness at one of the rare meetings between the two said that Lincoln kept referring to Truth pejoratively as "aunty," just "as he would his washerwoman."[279]

Sojourner Truth.

Clearly the two were not friends; not even casual acquaintances. Since Lincoln—who spent his entire adult life pushing for the deportation of blacks[280]—repeatedly ignored Truth's complaints about his poor treatment of African-Americans,[281] it would be more accurate to say that the two were adversaries. This was the same relationship he had with thousands of others from what he called the "inferior race."[282]

QUESTION: Why do Liberals and even many uninformed Conservatives idolize 19th-Century Virginia slave Nat Turner, even creating worshipful books and films about him?
ANSWER: As with all Yankee myths and their central themes and figures, this one too serves its purpose: to confuse and mislead the public while veiling the truth about the American Civil War. And what was the truth about Nat Turner?

Far from being the iconic hero of abolition, as Turner is portrayed in the North, he was actually a deranged black racist and violent psychopath who placed little value on human life, particularly if that human life happened to have white skin. He certainly proved this when, on August 21 and 22, 1831, inspired by the false and malign writings of Massachusetts South-hater William Lloyd Garrison, Turner recruited a gang of fellow black supremacists, who eagerly roamed the Virginia countryside for two days murdering white families—most of whom were non-slave owners.[283]

The Nat Turner Massacre.

Using "quiet" instruments to avoid detection, such as hatchets and knives, Turner intentionally chose to kill whites in their sleep. As he and his mob snuck from house to house in the dead of night, no one was spared, not even women, children, and newborn infants. Included among the slain was his own master, Joseph Travers, and his entire family. Why? Travers was known to be a gentle, benevolent, religious man to all, including Turner. Over the next forty-eight hours some fifty-five whites were viciously slaughtered[284] before Turner was captured (cowering in a cave), arrested, tried, and finally hanged on November 11, 1831, in Jerusalem, Virginia.[285]

This is the man worshiped by the Left, set up as an idol for massacring helpless innocent white Southerners.

Liberals can write a thousand adoring books and make a thousand reverential movies about Turner; they can alter his story, change his character, and even completely revise antebellum history (all which they have actually done). But it will not change the truth.

Here in the traditional South, where facts are more important than political correctness, personal ideologies, and "social justice," Turner is still regarded as the Devil incarnate; a fiendish monster whose name will forever live in infamy.[286]

SIX

THE

CONSTITUTION

MULTIPLE CHOICE: How many constitutions has America had?
A. 1.
B. 2.
C. 3.
D. 4.

ANSWER: C. Our three constitutions are: 1) The Articles of Confederation (1781-1789); 2) The Constitution of the United States of America (1788-present); 3) The Constitution of the Confederate States of America (1861-1865).

TRUE OR FALSE: Our first constitution, The Articles of Confederation, was replaced by the U.S. Constitution because the central government the Articles created was deemed too weak to govern adequately.

ANSWER: True. After living under the Articles of Confederation for several years many politicians, mainly Liberals, came to believe that the central government was not strong enough. It had not been given the power to levy taxes, interpret laws, or regulate foreign trade, for instance.[287] Nearly all political power had been assigned to the individual states, a conservative type of government that is known as a confederation or confederacy (a weak central government supported by strong sovereign states), hence the name of our first constitution, "The Articles of Confederation." Against the wishes of our more conservative Founders, men such as Patrick Henry, the U.S. Constitution was drawn

Patrick Henry.

up to make the central government more powerful. It went into operation in 1789, officially replacing the Articles.

Tragically, the U.S. central government has continued to grow in size, strength, and power ever since, completely altering the original model intended by the Founding Generation. From its inception as a confederacy *with no federal governmental departments or bureaus*, it evolved into a confederate republic. Yet, even against the warning of the Founders, it is moving closer and closer toward nationhood, the nightmare of our country's small government conservative creators and the dream of our country's big government liberal activists.[288] According to the U.S. government itself, as of this writing (2017), a staggering 659 departments and bureaus are now under its operation.[289]

TRUE OR FALSE: Liberals have always loved and honored the U.S. Constitution.

ANSWER: False. Progressives, who by nature loathe limited government, have a long history of disrespect and revilement toward the U.S. Constitution. Their abuses are legendary and began even as its ink was drying in 1787.

Left-leaning Founding Father Alexander Hamilton, for example, referred to the Constitution as "weak,"[290] "a frail and worthless fabric,"[291] while John Adams (another Liberal, then known misleadingly as a "Federalist") had such a low opinion of it that he assumed it would disappear within a generation.[292] A half century later radical Liberal William Lloyd Garrison burned the Constitution in the public square.[293] Lincoln's own Liberal compatriots called it a "scrap of paper," a "covenant with death

Alexander Hamilton.

and a league with hell,"[294] and "a thing of nothing, which must be changed."[295]

In our own time big government Liberal Barack Hussein Obama followed in the footsteps of his 19th-Century predecessors, referring to the Constitution as "an imperfect document," while his anti-American followers eagerly campaigned to throw out the entire thing, calling it "old, outdated, and useless."[296]

As a leftist, Lincoln, who began his political life as a Whig (Liberal),[297] was no different than Obama and every other leftist on this particular score. In February 1861, while meeting with a Southern peace commission at Willard's Hotel in Washington, D.C., the president-elect was asked by New York businessman William E. Dodge what he was going to do to prevent war with the South.

Lincoln's response is chilling: "When I get to the Oval Office, I shall take an oath to the best of my ability to preserve, protect, and defend the Constitution. This is a great and solemn duty. With the support of the people and the assistance of the Almighty I shall undertake to perform it. I have full faith that I shall perform it. It is not the Constitution as I would like to have it, but as it is that is to be defended."[298]

Abraham Lincoln.

Reading between the lines, it is obvious that even prior to becoming president, Lincoln was plotting to alter, and even destroy, the carefully constructed government of Thomas Jefferson, James Madison, James Monroe, Thomas Paine, Elbridge Gerry, George Mason, Patrick Henry, and the other *conservative* Founders.[299]

Why do Liberals in general have an undying disdain for our country's most sacred document? Because *the U.S. Constitution has a conservative foundation*, one intended to limit the size, power, and reach of the federal government. For it was first imagined by highly educated conservatives, created by common-sense traditionalists, and written out largely by a Conservative (then known as an Antifederalist), James Madison, later to become our fourth president.[300]

QUESTION: The majority of 19th-Century Liberals believed that there was something greater than the Constitution, something that was more important than the Constitution, something that superseded it. What was it?

Franklin Delano Roosevelt.

ANSWER: Victorian progressives called it "higher law," and it is the same thing that 21st-Century progressives call "social justice."

"Social justice" is a purely subjective concept, of course, which gives Liberals wide latitude in its use and definition. In essence the Liberal view of life is a socialist, atheist, pessimistic one: the world is a dark cruel place filled with a myriad of evils (capitalism, sexism, misogyny, racism, patriarchy, theology, masculinism, power, privilege, microaggressions, etc.). These stifle the happiness of the common man and woman, whose lives are filled with woe, despair, struggle, and suffering due to "bigoted greedy capitalists."

The cure? In the eyes of Liberals the downtrodden uneducated masses are helpless victims who cannot survive without *government*, which must use its executive, judicial, and legislative powers to impose "social justice" on the masses in order to compensate for life's inherent inequities. The price? Personal freedom. The people are tricked into giving up their liberty in exchange for governmental support, and this support can only come by way of unlimited big government, with its oppressive rules, heavy taxes, and Big Brother style authoritarianism.

Because the Constitution is largely a conservative document whose primary purpose is to restrict the size and growth of government, progressives had to come up with a ploy to get around it. And that ploy was "higher law," an "unwritten constitution" based on the nebulous indefinable idea of, in modern terms, "social justice." In this way Victorian Liberals sought to displace and override the real Constitution, favoring government slavery over chattel slavery.

Here we have the antebellum foundation of the American Civil War, that great clash between Northern liberalism and its loose interpretation of the Constitution, and Southern conservatism and its strict interpretation of the Constitution.[301]

SEVEN

THE SOUTHERN CONFEDERACY

TRUE OR FALSE: The Southern Confederacy of 1861 was America's first confederacy.

ANSWER: False.   Native-Americans were forming confederacies thousands of years before the arrival of the first Europeans. [302]

The Declaration of Independence.

MULTIPLE CHOICE: The Southern Confederacy was America's

A. first European confederacy.

B. second European confederacy.

C. third European confederacy.

D. fourth European confederacy.

ANSWER: B. Our *first* European-American confederacy was the United States of America, which the Founders purposefully created as a confederation. [303] Hence, our first constitution was called "The Articles of Confederation." Numerous presidents (including Lincoln), as well as thousands of politicians and statesmen, continued to refer to the U.S. as "the confederacy," "our confederacy," or "the American confederacy" well into the mid 1800s. [304]

TRUE OR FALSE: Southerners made up the name "The Confederate States of America," which is why it has no connection to the U.S.A.

ANSWER: False. The name "The Confederate States of America" is integrally associated with the U.S.A., and for good reason: it was one of the most popular nicknames for the U.S.A. throughout the 18th and 19th Centuries. It was so well-known and accepted at the time that it was used by both Americans and foreigners.[305]

Here we have more proof that the Southern states seceded, not to "overthrow the Union" or to "save slavery," as Liberal authors maintain, but to preserve the original government and constitution created by the U.S. Founding Fathers. This is also why the Southern Confederacy, or C.S.A., even patterned her constitution and her first national flag on those of the U.S.A.[306] With its rich and relevant history and long ties to the Founders and the first U.S. government, the name "Confederate States of America" was an appropriate one for the seceding Southern states indeed.[307]

FILL IN THE BLANKS: The Southern Confederacy, the C.S.A., is still a _____ _____ government.
ANSWER: "living legitimate." This is because it was not "destroyed," as Yankee myth teaches. It was never "closed down," never officially made "nonexistent." Thus it is still a lawful, viable, constitutionally created republic.

It is true that Confederate General Robert E. Lee signed Union General Ulysses S. Grant's "surrender agreement" on April 9, 1865. But even though he was the highest ranking Rebel military officer at the time, Lee lacked the authority to make such a momentous political decision. The Confederate Congress, the only body with such power, never signed a single sheet of paper authorizing the termination of the Confederate government, the permanent suspension of the Confederate Constitution, or the dissolution of the Confederate States.

All are technically still intact and active, awaiting the right time and the right individuals to relaunch what St. George Tucker called the "Confederate Republic," Thomas Jefferson's "lasting Confederacy"; what Tocqueville and many others called "The Confederate States of America"—the government originally intended by the U.S. Founding Fathers.[308]

TRUE OR FALSE: Jefferson Davis was America's first and only *Confederate* president.

Samuel Huntington.

ANSWER: False. During America's confederation period, 1781-1789, there were ten presidents who served prior to George Washington—who was the first president to serve under the United States Constitution. Our first ten presidents were known by the title "President of the United States in Congress Assembled," and, as specified in Article 9 of the Articles of Confederation, each presidential term was limited to one year. (Several men served partial terms, otherwise there would have only been eight U.S. Confederate presidents). Here are their names in order of service:

1. President Samuel Huntington of Connecticut: served from September 28, 1779, to July 6, 1781.
2. President Thomas McKean of Delaware: served from July 10, 1781, to November 4, 1781.
3. President John Hanson of Maryland: served from November 5, 1781, to November 4, 1782.
4. President Elias Boudinot of New Jersey: served from November 4, 1782, to November 3, 1783.
5. President Thomas Mifflin of Pennsylvania: served from November 3, 1783, to June 3, 1784.
6. President Richard Henry Lee of Virginia: served from November 30, 1784, to November 23, 1785.
7. President John Hancock of Massachusetts: served from November 23, 1785, to June 6, 1786.
8. President Nathaniel Gorham of Massachusetts: served from June 6, 1786, to November 13, 1786.
9. President Arthur St. Clair of Pennsylvania: served from February 2, 1787, to October 29, 1787.
10. President Cyrus Griffin of Virginia: served from January 22, 1788, to March 4, 1789.[309]

EIGHT

THE AMERICAN

UNION

TRUE OR FALSE: The American Union was meant to be perpetual.
ANSWER: False. The word "perpetual" does not appear in the U.S. Constitution, and for good reason: the American Union, the U.S.A., was formed by the Founding Fathers as a "*voluntary*" alliance,[310] a "friendly association" of states held together by "good faith" and the "exchanges of equity and comity"—not physical force.[311]

A voluntary union of sovereign political bodies is defined as a confederacy or confederation, which is precisely what the Founders called the U.S., whose first constitution they very consciously named "The Articles of Confederation."

As for the concept of the U.S. being a "perpetual union," this is nothing but a fantasy concocted by American Liberals and socialists to further their government- and nation-building agenda.[312]

Minutemen.

TRUE OR FALSE: The Founding Fathers never intended the U.S.A. to be a nation.
ANSWER: True. The original design of the U.S. was a confederacy, a small limited central government operating under the auspices of a group of all-powerful sovereigns which the Founders referred to as "nation-states,"[313] "little republics,"[314] or "distinct nations."[315] As the states themselves were considered little nations in their own right, it is obvious that the U.S.A. was not meant to be a nation.

Samuel Adams.

The Founding Fathers, in fact, formally rejected the idea of nationhood, and we have record of their decision. On December 3, 1787, in considering the formulation of the new U.S. Constitution, Samuel Adams hesitated, for it seem weighted in favor of a national government rather than the sovereignty of the states: "I stumble at the threshold. I meet with a *national government*, instead of a *federal [confederate] union of sovereign states*. . . . If the several states are to become one entire nation, under one legislature, its powers to extend to all legislation, and its laws to be supreme, and control the whole, the idea of sovereignty in these states must be lost."[316]

The Founders, ever concerned about governmental consolidation and the subsequent loss of state sovereignty, carefully distinguished between a large national government (a nation) and a small federal government (a confederacy).[317] At the Philadelphia Convention in 1787—where big government Liberals like Alexander Hamilton had pushed for a "consolidation of the Sovereignties of the several States in[to] one single grand Republic"[318]—one of them, William Patterson of New Jersey, correctly asserted that "the amendment of the confederacy was the object of all the laws and commissions upon the subject. . . . The commissions under which we act are not only the measure of our power, they denote, also, the sentiments of the states on the subject of our deliberation. The idea of a *national government* [nation], as contradistinguished from a *federal one* [confederacy], never entered into the mind of any of them [the states]; and to the public mind we must accommodate ourselves. . . . *We are met here*

Alexander Hamilton.

as deputies of thirteen independent sovereign states, for federal [confederate] purposes. Can we consolidate their sovereignty, and form one nation, and *annihilate the sovereignty of our states*, who have sent us here for other purposes? . . . But it is said that this national government is to act on individuals, and not on states; and cannot a federal [confederate] government be so formed as to operate in the same way? It surely may. I therefore declare that I will never consent to the present system, and I shall make all the interest against it, in the state I represent, that I can."[319]

QUESTION: In April 1861 why did the Union (then being governed by Liberals—at that time the Republicans) want to wipe out states' rights in the South?

ANSWER: Because Liberals, whose primary goal is to establish big government, cannot turn the U.S. into one large "indivisible nation" if the individual states are considered little "nations," with the power to ignore or override the decisions and activities of the central government (known as "nullification").[320] This, in turn, is why early American liberals, socialists, and communists loathed the conservative, states rights loving South—and it is why modern ones still do.[321]

FILL IN THE BLANK: Civil War Liberals (Republicans) wanted to replace chattel slavery with _____ slavery.

ANSWER: "government." To this day big government-obsessed progressives tacitly promote the idea of the enslavement of the American people by the federal government. Conservatives, on the other hand, openly promote the idea of personal freedom, self-government, and constitutional protections of individual and states' rights.

U.S. Capitol Building, Washington, D.C.

NINE

SLAVERY

TRUE OR FALSE: Only modern blacks descend from slaves.

ANSWER: False. Slavery has been found on every continent and among nearly every people and society dating back to the beginning of recorded history. Indeed, slavery must be considered the foundation of civilization, for without it cities and large scale farming would have never come into being, and these in turn provided leisure time for the creation of culture (literature, art, music).

Vikings enslaving fellow Europeans, 8th Century.

In short, there is no known race or nationality that has not practiced slaving, slave trading, or slavery, nearly all who began by enslaving their own people. This means that everyone reading these words, no matter what color your skin is or where you are from, has ancestors who were both slave owners and slaves. We are all descendants of slavery.[322]

MULTIPLE CHOICE: On which continent has slavery been practiced the longest?

A. Europe.
B. The Americas.
C. Asia.
D. Africa.
E. Australia.

ANSWER: D. The earliest known records of slavery come from Africa, where it has been practiced for at least 5,000 years. By 500 B.C. Africans were exporting their own people as slaves. This was 1,000

African chief enslaving fellow African.

years before the start of the transatlantic slave trade with Europe and the Americas. The practice of various forms of indigenous slavery, many of them extremely inhumane, is still common across Africa.[323]

TRUE OR FALSE: The American slave trade got its start in the South.

ANSWER: False. The American slave trade got its start in the North, in Massachusetts to be exact, in the year 1638, when the first group of African slaves were brought into Boston Harbor aboard the New England slaving ship *Desire*.[324]

TRUE OR FALSE: American slavery got its start in the North.
ANSWER: True. American slavery, which is connected to but distinct from the American slave trade, began in 1641 when Massachusetts became the first of the original 13 states (colonies) to legalize and monetize it.[325]

TRUE OR FALSE: The South was a massive slave trade center, with Southern slave ships leaving for Africa everyday from Southern slave ports. Millions of Africans were made into American slaves in this way by the South.
ANSWER: False. Not a single slave ship ever sailed from the South, for the South did not engage in the transatlantic slave trade, and therefore did not own or operate slave vessels or enslave a single African. The American slave trade was, in fact, exclusively a Yankee enterprise, with some of the more important slave ports being in Massachusetts, Pennsylvania, Rhode Island, New Jersey, Connecticut, and Washington, D.C. In contrast the

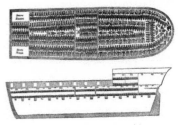
Deck of Yankee slave ship.

South had no slave ports.[326]

America's slave capitol was the state of New York, which was founded by the Dutch in 1624 to serve as a slaving hub due to its central proximity between the Northern and the Southern states.[327] New York City was founded to serve as the state's primary slave seaport. From here the Dutch hoped to maximize slave sales and further spread their slave trading business throughout the Eastern seaboard.[328]

QUESTION: Which state practiced slavery the longest?
ANSWER: New York, a true slave regime or slavocracy, was so entrenched in the institution that it was involved far longer than any other state: 239 years.[329] Vestiges of its long and lucrative involvement in slavery are obvious today: New York City is not only America's largest city but also our country's financial center.[330]

MULTIPLE CHOICE: Which region of the country had the most slaves in the year 1776?
A. The South.
B. The North.
C. The East.
D. The West.
ANSWER: B. In 1776, at the time of the formation of the *first* Confederate States of America, the U.S.A., of the 500,000 slaves in the 13 colonies, 300,000 (or 60 percent) were possessed by the Northern ones, only 200,000 (or 40 percent) by the Southern ones. It was only later, when Yankee slave traders actively pushed slavery even further south, that Dixie came to possess more slaves than the North.[331]

Southern "slave."

TRUE OR FALSE: The South always had a higher percentage of slave owners than the North.
ANSWER: False. Records from the early 1700s reveal that 42 percent of all New York households owned slaves, and that the share of slaves in both New York and New Jersey was larger than that of North Carolina.

In some Northern cities nearly 100 percent of the inhabitants were slave owners.[332]

Contrast this with the Old South, where at no time did individual white slave owners make up more than 4.8 percent of the total population (only 25 percent of Southern households possessed one or more slaves), the peak number in 1860. And as one moves further back in time these figures sharply decrease. In fact, in most Southern towns there were no slave owners.[333]

QUESTION: In the American Civil War why did millions of people fight over slavery?
ANSWER: Let us rephrase the question. Would you be willing to sacrifice your life and even the lives of your family, as well as risk your home, your job, your neighborhood, your town, and even your state to destroy or preserve an institution that was both legal and only practiced by a handful of people? Would you be willing to topple the stock market and bankrupt the government treasury for an institution that few actually cared about? Would you be willing to create millions of refugees and instigate nationwide unemployment for an institution that everyone already knew was on the verge of extinction?

Of course not! And the same was true of Victorian Americans. It is time to bury this age-old Northern lie in the Cemetery of Yankee Myths once and for all.[334]

TRUE OR FALSE: Authentic slavery was never practiced in the American South.
ANSWER: True. Slavery is the state of working under the control, ownership, or absolute dominion of another, without pay, and often for life. Additionally, slaves have almost no rights of any kind, are generally debased and disenfranchised, and cannot purchase their freedom. In short, a true slave is seen by his or her owner as little different than a cow or a horse, just another piece of livestock to be owned and worked until he or she is no longer useful.[335]

Servitude, on the other hand, is for a limited duration, the individual is not "owned" (his boss is not his "owner" or "master," but rather his employer), he is paid a wage, and he may hire himself out to work for others. Servants also possess a wide variety of personal and civil rights that are both recognized and protected by society and tempered by religious sentiment. In this way, under servitude a person's right to comfort and happiness are taken for granted and he or she is treated with common respect and decency.[336] Finally, and most significantly, servants have the right and the power to buy their freedom.[337]

By definition then authentic slavery was never practiced in the Old South. What was practiced was a mild form of indentured servitude. And it was only indentured because the servant (known wrongly in the North as a "slave") had to first pay off his indenture (the cost of his purchase) before his service was considered complete. Any Southern "slave" could buy his or her freedom in this way, and thousands did just that. This actually makes the South's version of the "peculiar institution" a combination of apprenticeship and indentured servitude.[338]

MULTIPLE CHOICE: What noted American black "slaves" purchased their freedom, proving that Southern slavery was *not* true slavery, but servitude?
A. Abolitionist and civil rights leader Frederick Douglass.
B. Black racist-militant Denmark Vesey.

C. Travel adventurer Gustavus Vassa.
D. Abraham Lincoln's modiste, Elizabeth Keckley (who purchased her freedom with money she made hiring herself out as a dressmaker).
ANSWER: All of the above.[339]

TRUE OR FALSE: Africans were not the only slaves in early America.
ANSWER: True. European-Americans, Native-Americans, and Asian-Americans were all once

Elizabeth Keckley.

enslaved by other races between the 1600s and the 1800s. White slavery in particular has been almost wholly ignored by the mainstream, for it does not fit into the fake American history invented by Liberals.[340]

One of the most obvious and dramatic historical events proving white slavery in Africa, as one example, were the Barbary Wars, fought in the early 1800s between the U.S. and several North African states—in great part an attempt by America (and also Europe) to free some 1.5 million whites that had been enslaved by Africans.[341]

TRUE OR FALSE: Europeans were not the only slave owners in early America.
ANSWER: True. Native-Americans were major slave owners from the pre-colonial period right up to the Civil War. In the beginning they enslaved one another, but quickly turned to enslaving Europeans and Africans after these two races began arriving in the early 1600s.[342]

Since Africa has a long history of domestic slavery (she began selling and exporting her own people as early as 500 B.C.), and because she has practiced slavery longer than any other region on earth, it is not surprising to learn that African-Americans took to slave owning early on. Indeed, the first official American slave owner was a black man by the name of Anthony Johnson. The Virginia slaver from Angola (Africa), who owned both black and white slaves,[343] actually helped launch the American slave trade by forcing authorities to legally define the meaning of "slave ownership."[344]

Native-Americans enslaving a European-American woman.

TRUE OR FALSE: There could not have been more than a few black slave owners in early America.
ANSWER: False. At least 25 percent of all free African-Americans, both North and South, were slave owners before the Civil War. In Charleston, South Carolina, alone, between the years 1820 and 1840, 75 percent of the city's free blacks owned slaves. Nearly all black Southern slave owners, many who owned both black and white slaves, were not only proslavery and anti-abolition, they were also pro-Confederacy, and fought as courageously for the Southern Cause as white Southerners.[345]

Some, like the African-American Metoyers, an anti-abolition family from Louisiana, owned huge numbers of black slaves; in their case, at least 400. At about $1,500 a piece their servants were worth a total of $600,000, or $20 million in today's currency. This made the Metoyers among the wealthiest people in the U.S., black or white, then or now. Louisiana's all-black Confederate army unit, the Augustin Guards, was named after the family patriarch, Augustin Metoyer.[346]

The Underground Railroad.

QUESTION: What made the Underground Railroad so successful?

ANSWER: In modern terms the Underground Railroad was not successful, and, in fact, like the system itself, statistics surrounding it have been greatly exaggerated and romanticized. Though the Railroad functioned throughout most of the War, only about 2,000 slaves (just 500 servants a year) out of 4.5 million (North and South) availed themselves of it—a mere 0.04 percent of the total. Some reckon there were as many as 4,000 total (1,000 Southern slaves a year), but this would still be only 0.08 percent of the total.[347]

There was no *literal* Underground Railroad, of course: it was not underground, it was not a railroad, and it was not even secret. Ineffective, disorganized, and inefficient, it served mainly as a psychological crutch for a few Yankee liberals and abolitionists who wanted to believe that they were helping to end slavery.[348]

QUESTION: The Old South is known for its violent abuse of its slaves. Is this true?

ANSWER: Of course not. Just as violence is illegal today, violence against one's black servants, in any form, was illegal across the

Slave abuse was rare, illegal, and socially unacceptable in the Old South.

Old South, and those few owners who abused their chattel faced stiff penalties. Most were turned in by concerned neighbors. Punishments ranged from fines to actual execution for more serious offences. Such intolerance for the inhumane treatment of slaves is to be expected in the region of the country where the American abolition movement was launched in the 1700s.[349]

FILL IN THE BLANKS: The North's treatment of her slaves was _____ _____ than the South's treatment of hers.

ANSWER: "far worse." Though our mainstream history books tell us that Southern slave owners were "extremely cruel," and daily whipped, beat, raped, tortured, and even murdered their human chattel without fear of reprisal, this is false. The region where such outrages were most likely to be committed was in the far less racially tolerant Old North.

In New York, for example, where a 1702 law authorized masters to chastise their human chattel at their own discretion, slaves convicted of heinous crimes, such as murder, were subject to all manner of hideous

fates. These included being "burned at the stake," "gibbeted alive," and "broken on the wheel." This is precisely what occurred in 1712, when New York authorities hanged 13 slaves, burned four of them alive (one over a "slow fire"), "broke" one on the wheel, and left another to starve to death chained to the floor. In 1741 the Empire State executed 31 blacks: 13 were burned at the stake, 18 were hanged, while another 71 were transported out of state.[350]

On another occasion a New York slave named Tom, found guilty of killing two people, was ordered to be "roasted over a slow fire so that he will suffer in torment for at least eight to ten hours." Such executions were often performed in public, in full view of ordinary New Yorkers. While this was going on, Southern states like South Carolina were banning the

Public slave burning, New York City, New York.

public punishment of blacks. The naturally humanitarian Southerner found such scenes "distressing," quite unlike his more thick-skinned Yankee compatriot to the North.[351]

QUESTION: If the North really started the American slave trade and practiced slavery for hundreds of years, where is the evidence?

ANSWER: Since Northern slavery started *before* Southern slavery, it is older, and thus most of it is buried far beneath the ground, and its artifacts are less well preserved and more difficult

Yankee slave skeletons.

to find. Despite this problem, archaeological proof of Northern slavery is being brought to light like never before.

Near Salem, Massachusetts, for instance, scientists have uncovered traces of a 13,000 acre plantation once owned by a Yankee named Samuel Browne. Near Browne's farm, one that traded its products for Caribbean rum and molasses, a massive slave cemetery was discovered, the final resting place of some 100 African-American slaves who worked there between the years 1718 and 1780. More and more Northern slave plantations and slave cemeteries, like these, are being discovered and excavated each year, making it more and more difficult for the anti-South movement to hide the truth about Lincoln's War.[352]

There are more obvious traces of Yankee slavery, however, and one of these is the pineapple symbol, commonly seen decorating front doors, gates, store fronts, street signs, and driveways. Though the emblem of

Pineapple "welcome" motif: symbol of Yankee slavery.

the pineapple is now seen as a "welcome" sign across America, this is an intentional corruption to mask its original meaning: when New England slave traders returned from their ocean expeditions to the tropics to pick up slaves, they would impale a pineapple on their fencepost to let the townspeople know that they were "welcome" to come in and shop for both slave products and for slaves themselves.[353]

TEN

ABOLITION

Southern slave owner voluntarily freeing his servants.

QUESTION: Where did the American abolition movement start? **ANSWER:** In the South, where the first voluntary manumission in the American colonies took place in Virginia in 1655.[354] While Yankees, the founders of American slavery, were busy building up the slave trade throughout the Northern states, Southerners were hard at work trying to come up with a plan to abolish the institution. Foremost among the better known Southern abolitionists were Thomas Jefferson, George Washington, George Mason, James Madison, James Monroe, and St. George Tucker.[355]

Virginian Patrick Henry summed up the feelings of most Southerners when he asked, how can anyone seriously believe "that I am a master of slaves of my own purchase? I am drawn along by the general inconvenience of living here without them. I will not—I can not justify it! I believe a time will come when an opportunity will be offered to abolish this lamentable evil. Every thing we can do is to improve it, if it happens in our day; if not, let us transmit to our descendants, together with our slaves, a pity for their unhappy lot, and an abhorrence of slavery."[356]

TRUE OR FALSE: All of America's abolition societies were in the North. There were never any in the South.
ANSWER: False. Of the 130 abolition societies established before 1827 by Northern abolitionist Benjamin Lundy, over 100, comprising four-fifths of the total membership, were in the South. Southern

Benjamin S. Hedrick.

Quakers were among the first to come out against the spread of the institution. Early North Carolina, as another example, had a number of well-known "forceful" antislavery leaders, such as Benjamin Sherwood Hedrick and Daniel Reaves Goodlow. And in South Carolina the famed Quaker sisters Sarah and Angelina Grimké were just two among millions of Southerners fighting for the cause of abolition. The Southern abolition movement involved so many Southerners, so many Southern states, and covered such a large span of time, that the latter wrote an entire book on the subject.[357]

QUESTION: Why did the South not emancipate her slaves before the Civil War?

ANSWER: The South, the birthplace of the American abolition movement, had been working on the complete destruction of slavery for centuries. In 1831 the American abolition movement was at its peak in Dixie when William Lloyd Garrison began antagonizing the South for its involvement in the institution—this despite the fact that he was from Massachusetts, the state that started both the American slave trade and American slavery! For the first time Yankees began to demand "immediate, total, and unconditional abolition" in the South. But this was easier said than done, as millions of lives and dollars were at stake. Thomas Jefferson perceptively referred to the hazards of abolition as "holding a wolf by the ear," for either way (abolition or keeping slavery), there were numerous hazards involved.[358]

Much earlier the South had made up its mind to gradually emancipate its slaves. This meant abolishing the institution over time so that both owners and slaves could adjust to the massive social and financial

William L. Garrison.

changes that abolition would bring. But radical Liberals like Garrison would not accept this. Even though the Northern states had given themselves hundreds of years to gradually emancipate their slaves, they refused to grant the same courtesy to the Southern states. Not wanting to be told what to do by their arrogant meddling neighbors to the North, the South dug in its heels on the topic of slavery. Not in defense of it, as mainstream history books falsely claim, but in defense of *gradual* emancipation. The South would decide for herself what to do about slavery in her region and in her own time and way—and that was final.[359]

The famed Yankee slave ship, *Nightingale*.

Naturally the bossy nosy North would not listen, and instead used "the problem of Southern slavery" to foment hatred and intolerance toward Dixie. Though slavery was not the cause of the Civil War, 30 years later this very issue would be maliciously used by many Liberals to justify it. To hide the truth about the conflict, the "slavery was the cause of the Civil War" myth entered our history books as "fact," one of the greatest scams ever perpetrated on the world.[360]

FILL IN THE BLANKS: The real reason radical Northern Liberals demanded "immediate, total, and unconditional abolition" in the South had nothing to do with black civil rights. According to Southerners living at the time, in reality it was nothing more than _____ _____, simple jealously over the South's wealth, prestige, and power.
ANSWER: "social spite." This was attested to by millions.[361]

TRUE OR FALSE: America's "Great Emancipator" was Abraham Lincoln.
ANSWER: False. To begin with, Lincoln was a self-evident white racist, white supremacist, and white separatist, which is why he stalled the Emancipation Proclamation for as long as possible, then only issued it reluctantly—later even regretting it.[362] Little wonder: it was first received by the general public with suspicion, disgust, and anger, for it

clearly had nothing to do with black civil rights.[363] It was merely another cynical tool Northern Liberals and socialists intended to use to destroy states' rights in the South, resist the conservative party, and consolidate political power in Washington.[364]

Second, the Emancipation Proclamation was illegal and therefore useless, meaningless, and powerless. As a result, not a single slave North or South was freed by it. Official abolition only came nearly a year after Lincoln's death, in December 1865, with the ratification of the Thirteenth Amendment. Thus he does not come close to qualifying for the title the "Great Emancipator."[365] In fact, Lincoln would be more accurately described as the "Great Impersonator."[366]

Our country's first *real* Great Emancipator was a Southerner, Robert Carter III of Nomini Hall in Virginia, who voluntarily freed his 500 slaves in 1791 at a loss of $15 million in today's currency.[367]

TRUE OR FALSE: The North abolished slavery before the South did. **ANSWER:** False. Anti-South writers tell us that the Northern states "abolished slavery completely by the early 1800s," but this is an outright lie. In reality the North never abolished slavery. This term, pertaining to Yankee slavery, is in truth a misnomer then. What the Northern states actually did was merely suppress the institution until, over time, it naturally faded away due to neglect, unprofitability, and ultimately white Yankee racism. This was accomplished through a slow and voluntarily process; one, it should be emphasized, that took place without any interference from the South.[368]

Yankee slavers separating a slave family, something almost unknown in the South.

ELEVEN
RACISM

TRUE OR FALSE: White racism was more severe in the Old South than in the Old North.

ANSWER: False. Thousands of eyewitness testimonies have come down to us revealing the exact opposite; namely that racism was far more acute in the North than in the South. This phenomenon was noted by both Northerners and Southerners, Americans and foreigners. One from the latter group was Englishman James Silk Buckingham, who, in the 1840s, wrote that "the prejudice of colour is not nearly so strong in the South as in the North."[369]

Alexis de Tocqueville.

Another keen observer of 19th-Century America was French diplomat Alexis de Tocqueville. After traveling throughout the U.S. in the early 1800s he recorded the following: "Whosoever has inhabited the United States must have perceived that in those parts of the Union in which the negroes are no longer slaves, they have in nowise drawn nearer to the whites. On the contrary, the prejudice of the race appears to be stronger in the States which have abolished slavery [the North] than in those where it still exists [the South]; and nowhere is it so intolerant as in those States where servitude never has been known [the West]."[370]

MULTIPLE CHOICE: Black racism (black prejudice toward whites) during the American Civil War period was motivated primarily by
A. the old African belief that "only black skin is beautiful."
B. the black separatist movement.
C. ignorance and xenophobia.

D. the black nationalist movement.

E. the intentionally racially divisive policies of the Lincoln administration as well as the Republican Party (the Liberal party at the time) in general. This same divide-and-conquer ploy (intentionally stirring up racism by pitting the races against one another over make-believe issues) is used by Liberals (now Democrats) today. **ANSWER:** All of the above.[371]

Black African racism flourished in early America.

FILL IN THE BLANK: Abraham Lincoln is on record saying that he was a friend of, not African-Americans, but _____.
ANSWER: "colonization."[372] The black colonization movement was a Yankee-founded group whose goal was to deport African-Americans and "colonize" them in foreign lands.

MULTIPLE CHOICE: Which white Civil War officer called blacks "niggers" and was against black suffrage, interracial marriage, and even "associating" with non-whites?
A. Confederate General Nathan Bedford Forrest.
B. Union General William T. Sherman.
C. Confederate General John S. Mosby.
D. Union General Philip H. Sheridan.
ANSWER: B. Sherman had no love for African-Americans and never minced words on the subject.[373]

MULTIPLE CHOICE: Which top white political leader supported the idea of American apartheid and wanted each of the races to live in their own separate state?
A. Union Secretary of War Simon Cameron.
B. Confederate President Jefferson Davis.
C. Union President Abraham Lincoln.
D. Confederate Secretary of the Treasury Christopher G. Memminger.

ANSWER: C. Lincoln publicly announced his support of this idea on September 15, 1858, a little over two years before being elected president.[374]

MULTIPLE CHOICE: Which elected Civil War era official was fond of the "n" word, called *all* non-white people "inferior races," and was against black civil rights?
A. Confederate Vice President Alexander H. Stephens.
B. Union President Abraham Lincoln.
C. Confederate Secretary of State Robert A. Toombs.
D. Union Secretary of the Treasury Salmon P. Chase.
ANSWER: B. Lincoln made the following remark in September 1859, a little over one year before entering the White House: "Negro equality! Fudge!! How long, in the Government of a God great enough to make and maintain this universe, shall there continue [to be] knaves to vend and fools to gulp, so low a piece of demagoguism as this?"[375]

FILL IN THE BLANKS: With good reason Victorian Southerners asserted, and modern traditional Southerners still maintain, that Southern whites are the _____ _____ blacks have ever had in this country.
ANSWER: "best friends." Authentic history has repeatedly borne this truth out.[376]

MULTIPLE CHOICE: Which white Civil War officer told African-Americans that he viewed them as "brothers and sisters," and that they could always come to him for aid if ever they were ever in need?
A. Union General James S. Negley.
B. Confederate General Earl Van Dorn.
C. Union General Irvin McDowell.
D. Confederate General Nathan Bedford Forrest.
ANSWER: D. Forrest made this public comment before an all black audience in 1875.[377]

Nathan B. Forrest.

MULTIPLE CHOICE: African-Americans were prohibited from attending the funeral of which U.S. president?
A. Abraham Lincoln.
B. Millard Fillmore.
C. John Adams.
D. William Henry Harrison.
ANSWER: A. Abraham Lincoln.[378]

Southern slaves were considered legal "family members" of their white, black, red, or brown owners.

FILL IN THE BLANK: White racism was so entrenched in the Union army that eventually it had to be _____ due to complaints by black Yankee soldiers.
ANSWER: "banned." During inclement weather, for example, white Yankee soldiers were known to beat black Yankee soldiers, then push them out into the freezing night air in order to have the tents all to themselves. Name-calling and insults were also common.[379]

TRUE OR FALSE: African-Americans who refused to join the Union army were often whipped or even killed on the spot by Yankee recruiters.
ANSWER: True. The preferred Yankee methods of executing blacks who refused to "voluntarily" enlist were bayoneting and shooting. This type of violent racism was virtually unknown in the antebellum South.[380]

QUESTION: Who registered their slaves as legal "family members" at the time of purchase, Northerners or Southerners?
ANSWER: Southerners. This was a well-respected tradition in Dixie.[381]

QUESTION: Who registered their slaves as "property" at the time of purchase, Northerners or Southerners?
ANSWER: Northerners. Yankees put their African-American slaves on the same lists as farming equipment and other "merchandise," and taxed them as "livestock."[382]

TWELVE

WARTIME

PRISONS

TRUE OR FALSE: More Yankee POWs died in Southern prisons than Confederate POWs in Northern prisons.

ANSWER: False. This is what anti-South writers would like you to believe, for as part of what I call "The Great Yankee Coverup," this purposeful misrepresentation helps maintain the central lie about Lincoln's War; namely, that it was "necessary," "moral," and "justified." As educated students of the conflict know all too well, it was unnecessary, immoral, and unjustified.[383]

Edwin M. Stanton.

In fact, Lincoln's own Secretary of War Edwin M. Stanton stated that the reverse is true: a higher percentage of Southern POWs perished in Yankee prisons than Northern POWs in Confederate prisons.[384] Some estimate the Rebel prisoner loss to be as high as 200,000,[385] while the Yankee prisoner loss was closer to between 23,000[386] and 30,000.[387] Another Yankee myth dead and gone.[388]

TRUE OR FALSE: There were no bad Union prisons. All of the truly terrible jails were in the South.

ANSWER: False. There were numerous Union prisons with horrendous reputations and conditions, where thousands of Confederate POWs suffered frightful deaths. Among them were the Yankees' Johnson's Island Prison, known as the "Northern Andersonville";[389] Lincoln's gulag, the barbaric and overcrowded Fort Lafayette in New York Harbor;[390] and the New York Federal garrison called Elmira Prison (or "Hellmira," as inmates referred to it), where nearly 3,000 Confederates died unnecessarily.[391]

Benjamin J. Sweet.

Arguably the worst Union prison was Chicago's notorious Camp Douglas—a Yankee prison rightly referred to by all who witnessed it as "Eighty Acres of Hell." It was here that Yankee Colonel Benjamin J. Sweet tortured then purposefully starved to death nearly 6,000 Confederate prisoners.[392]

Why do we never hear about these Union prisons and accompanying atrocities? Because the victors, Liberal Yankees, wrote the history of the American Civil War, and chose to leave out anything and everything that made them look bad. Truly, as Walt Whitman once said, "the real war will never get in the books."[393]

Whitman was referring to mainstream books, however. Thankfully, the South is taking back her history, and independently-published books like this one are restoring the authentic facts for all to see.

THIRTEEN

EUROPEAN

SUPPORT

QUESTION: Why didn't Europe support the Confederacy?
ANSWER: Most of Europe did support the Confederacy, emotionally at least. The only reason she did not support the South officially was because she could not. Why? Lincoln threatened to go to war with any country who interfered with his invasion of Dixie. Thus Europe reluctantly remained "neutral," supporting the Confederacy from behind closed doors.[394]

James M. Mason (left), John Slidell (right).

TRUE OR FALSE: Europe stood squarely with Lincoln and the Union throughout the entire war.
ANSWER: False. Not once did Europe throw her support fully behind the U.S., and for a number of well documented reasons. As just one example, England, who was still smarting from losing the American colonies, was no friend of the U.S., and the recent search-and-seizure debacle known as the "Trent Affair"—in which two Confederate commissioners, James M. Mason (representative to St. James' Court in England) and John Slidell (representative to the French Court), had been taken by force in November 1861 by a U.S. sloop of war while traveling aboard the British ship *Trent*—had not helped matters. Their subsequent arrest and imprisonment created an international uproar, with France

aligning herself with England and the Confederacy. With both sides bristling, a war between England and the U.S. was only narrowly averted.

The Trent Affair was just one more reminder that the U.S. was not the true friend of either England or France, and as such could not be trusted. In fact, the incident only provoked more intense European sympathy for the Confederacy, particularly among the English.[395]

Queen Victoria.

MULTIPLE CHOICE: Which one of the following influential Europeans gave their support, in one form or another, to the Confederate States?
A. England's Queen Victoria.
B. France's Emperor Napoleon III.
C. England's Second Earl of Granville George Gower.
D. The Catholic Church's Pope Pius IX.
ANSWER: All of the above.[396]

TRUE OR FALSE: The main reason Europe refused to stand with the Confederacy was Southern slavery.
ANSWER: False. First, slavery was still legal and widely practiced across America's Northern states at the time.[397] Second, Europe herself made it clear that slavery had nothing to do with why she would not support Dixie.

In early 1865 Confederate President Jefferson Davis sent Louisiana Congressman Duncan F. Kenner on a secret mission to Britain with a proposal: the South would immediately emancipate her slaves in exchange for Britain's recognition. Prime Minister Henry John Temple, better known as Lord Palmerston, responded with an unwavering but friendly "no." Slavery was in no way preventing England from recognizing the legitimacy of the Confederacy.[398] Due to Lincoln's aggressive military threats toward Great Britain, there were no circumstances, the English statesman asserted, that could convince the British government to recognize the C.S.A. as an autonomous republic.[399]

In France Napoleon III stuck by Britain, stating that the issue of slavery had never once been taken into consideration concerning its decisions and reactions regarding the Confederacy.[400] Some French regions, Paris, for instance, where there were no active antislavery organizations, evinced little or no concern about slavery at all.[401]

Lord Palmerston.

Clearly, Lincoln was barking up the wrong tree by thinking that he could "obtain the favor of Europe" while preventing her from supporting the Confederacy over the issue of slavery.[402] As was so often the case, he was his own worst enemy in this regard: beginning with his First Inaugural Address on March 4, 1861, Lincoln had repeatedly promised not to interfere with Southern slavery,[403] while at the same time he continually assured the world that his one and only goal in invading Dixie was to "preserve the Union."[404]

Plainly, the War was not over slavery. Lincoln and the Northern people knew it, Davis and the Southern people knew it, and Queen Victoria, Napoleon, and the European people knew it.[405]

Charles Dickens.

In 1862 the truth about the American Civil War was aptly expressed by English novelist Charles Dickens, who wrote: "The Northern onslaught upon slavery is no more than a piece of specious humbug disguised to conceal its desire for economic control of the United States. Union means so many millions a year lost to the South; secession means loss of the same millions to the North. The love of money is the root of this as many, many other evils. The quarrel between the North and South is, as it stands, solely a fiscal quarrel."[406]

FOURTEEN
THE
KU KLUX KLAN

Reconstruction Klansmen.

TRUE OR FALSE: Today's Ku Klux Klan is the direct descendant of the post Civil War KKK. They're integrally connected, and are, in fact, the same organization.

ANSWER: False. Except for their name and regalia, the second or modern KKK, which formed in 1915, has no connection whatsoever with the first KKK, what I call the *Reconstruction KKK*, which was formed in December 1865, eight months after Lincoln's War ended. The only reason people think they are the same is ignorance of true history, as well as the mountain of disinformation that has been intentionally spread by uneducated South-haters about both organizations.[407]

QUESTION: Why did Confederate General Nathan Bedford Forrest found the KKK?

ANSWER: General Forrest did not found the KKK, for he was not introduced to the organization until around 1867, two years after it was formed. The names of the six men who did establish it on Christmas Eve 1865, in a haunted house in Pulaski, Tennessee, are well-known. They are: J. Calvin Jones, Captain John C. Lester, Richard R. Reed, Captain James R. Crowe, Frank O. McCord, and Captain John B. Kennedy.[408]

MULTIPLE CHOICE: The Reconstruction KKK was

A. a racist anti-black organization.

B. an anti-scallywag organization.

C. an anti-carpetbag organization.

D. a patriotic pro-Constitution organization made up primarily of Democrats, which at that time was America's Conservative party.

E. a social aid and welfare group dedicated to helping war widows, orphans, and Confederate veterans of any and all races.

ANSWER: B, C, D, and E.[409]

QUESTION: Why did the Reconstruction KKK only allow whites? **ANSWER:** The Reconstruction KKK allowed anyone of any race to join, as long as the individual obeyed their stringent rules and policies. This is why thousands of African-Americans, including black women, not only supported and aided the group, but started and operated their own all-black KKK chapters, such as the one in Nashville, Tennessee.[410] Under oath

African-American Klansmen, 1868.

Forrest himself testified that there were both white and black KKK members. There were KKK men in Tennessee and Mississippi "disguised, white men and negroes both," he said on the stand before the Joint Select Committee in 1871.[411]

TRUE OR FALSE: The chief weapon used by the Reconstruction KKK was violence. **ANSWER:** False. The chief weapon used by the Reconstruction KKK was fear. The organization was against violence of any kind, and only allowed it in cases of defense. In fact, violence was a violation of the rules of the Reconstruction KKK, and those who broke this law were subject to the death penalty.[412] In defending the Reconstruction KKK against this false charge Forrest himself said: "This Klan is not a political party; it is not a military party; it is a protective organization, and will never use violence except in resisting violence."[413]

Fear tactics were used primarily to scare carpetbaggers, scallywags, and other South-hating rascals out of the area, preferably out of the South altogether and back up North. Most of the terror engendered by the Reconstruction KKK was the result of their weird and unearthly looking garb, their strange unfathomable language, and their eerie writings and odd symbols and imagery. Unbeknownst to their victims, most of this was nonsensical and had no real meaning whatsoever. Yet it had the desired effect: in fear for their lives, most of the recipients of KKK threats sold their houses and moved out of town as soon as possible.[414]

William J. Simmons, founder of the modern KKK in 1915.

TRUE OR FALSE: The original KKK (1865) engaged in violent racist behavior and black lynchings, and therefore deserves the terrible reputation it has to this day.

ANSWER: False. The Reconstruction KKK was neither a racist or a violent organization. Both bigotry and physical force were against the constitution of the group, which is just one reason so many blacks and women supported and even joined the Reconstruction KKK. Forrest was adamant on this point, stating: "We are not the enemy of the blacks. . . . We reiterate that we are for peace and law and order. No man, white or black, shall be molested for his political sentiments."[415]

The reason the Reconstruction Klan has been smeared with the "violent racist" epithet is because of imposters; murderous men who wore the group's ghostly robes and frightening masks in an attempt to conceal their personal racial crimes and skullduggery from the law. These nefarious nonmembers did more to damage the reputation of the Reconstruction KKK than anything else, and the Klan drove them out wherever they were found.[416]

Tragically for both history and Dixie, due to the evil actions of a few deceivers, South-haters now ignorantly portray the entire Reconstruction KKK as a "racist, violent organization, based on white supremacy and white separatism." Just as erroneous they depict the old, first, or original KKK, the Reconstruction Ku Klux Klan, and the new, second, or modern KKK, the Knights of the Ku Klux Klan, as one and the same entity. In reality they are completely different in scope, purpose, functions, and mission, and former members of the Reconstruction KKK who lived to see the formation of the modern KKK in 1915 said as much.

It is unfortunate indeed that the founders of the modern Klan decided to borrow the name and unusual apparel of the older Reconstruction KKK. In doing so they themselves have helped further reenforce this false assumption, some even wrongly claiming direct descendancy from the original postwar Klan.[417]

TRUE OR FALSE: Confederate General Nathan Bedford Forrest was the first and only leader (known as the "Grand Wizard") of the entire KKK.

ANSWER: False. To begin with, no one knows who the real Grand Wizard was because, recording-keeping being forbidden by the group's constitution, the Reconstruction KKK never wrote anything down.[418] Secondly, since Forrest was not introduced to the group until two years after its formation, he could not have been either its founder or its "first and only leader."[419]

George W. Gordon.

The actual leader or Grand Wizard of the Reconstruction KKK was almost certainly former Confederate General George W. Gordon, a fact later testified to under oath by his wife Ora Gordon. Forrest himself denied even being a member, though he admitted that he supported the conservative patriotic organization. It is also worth noting that his many early biographers never mention any connection between the General and the Reconstruction KKK.[420]

Though several of the founders of the Reconstruction KKK later said that Forrest had been the Grand Wizard, these declarations cannot be taken seriously; especially in light of the bold fact that most contemporaries said that Forrest was *not* the Grand Wizard. After the

War the General was the most beloved, respected, and famous Confederate officer in Tennessee, the birthplace of the Reconstruction Klan. Having his name affiliated with the organization gave it added legality, authenticity, credibility, and panache, just as today celebrity names lend a product or group an air of dash, style, and legitimacy.[421]

At most Forrest was probably an advisor, and perhaps a part-time recruiter, for the Reconstruction KKK, who rightly saw the conservative organization as the best hope of restoring peace, safety, political order, and economic stability across the South.[422]

Because there are no surviving written chronicles of the Reconstruction KKK, because old memories are faulty at best, because celebrity is seductive, and because most testimonies given under oath are true, it is time to take Forrest, his biographers, and Mrs. Gordon at their word.[423]

The "Grand Ensign," the official flag of
the Reconstruction KKK, late 1860s.

FIFTEEN

THE

CONFEDERATE

FLAG

Confederate Battle Flag.

QUESTION: The South claims that the Confederate Battle Flag is not a symbol of slavery, racism, hatred, and treason. If this is true why do so many people think it is?

ANSWER: Only the ignorant and the brainwashed believe there is any link between "slavery, racism, hatred, and treason" and the Confederate Battle Flag.

The name itself debunks the false accusations of South-haters: the *Battle* Flag was a military ensign used on the battlefield. Its bright red background, blue cross, and white stars helped distinguish it from the U.S. Flag during the fog of war. What does such a banner have to do with slavery, and allegedly racism and hatred? Absolutely nothing![424] Besides, the American Civil War was not fought over slavery, as both Davis and Lincoln repeatedly declared, as the U.S. Congress stated, and as all of the major military officers on both sides frequently attested.[425]

As for the charge that the Confederate Battle Flag is "a symbol of treason," secession was legal in 1861 just as it was in 1776 at the time of the establishment of the U.S.A., a country that was literally founded on secession. Secession is legal to this day. If it were not we would know. For prohibiting secession would completely alter the nature of the U.S. government and its relationship to the states. Indeed, the government would become national, the Union would become a nation, and the states as independent sovereigns would disappear, forever "chaining" them to the national government.[426]

Plainly, this has not occurred. And it never will: as long as true patriots protect and preserve the *voluntary* union established by the Founding Fathers. If secession is banned and we become an *involuntary* union, we will no longer be the United States of America (plural). We will become the Consolidated American State (singular), moving steadfastly in the direction of communism.[427]

Saint Andrew's Cross.

TRUE OR FALSE: The Confederate Flag is an anti-Christian symbol.
ANSWER: False. The diagonal blue cross, or saltire, on the Confederate Battle Flag is the cross of Saint Andrew, the patron saint of Scotland. As it derives from the Christian flag of Christian Scotland, the Confederate Battle Flag, with its predominant Saint Andrew's Cross, could not be more Christian. It was carefully chosen, after all, by a deeply Christian section of a predominantly Christian country: the American South.[428]

TRUE OR FALSE: The South should be ashamed of the Confederate Flag.
ANSWER: False. Since the Confederate Flag is a Christian symbol representing the patriotic heritage and conservative history of the traditional South, there is nothing to be ashamed of. It is those who continually lie about the Confederate Flag for personal and political gain who should be ashamed. Our flag stays, and so it should.

TRUE OR FALSE: The Confederate Flag is used by various hate groups, therefore it's a symbol of hate.
ANSWER: False. One's personal view of an object does not mean that is what the object actually represents. The U.S. (American) Flag is also

used by hate groups, but we do not hear calls for its removal—and for good reason: like the Confederate Flag it is *not* a symbol of hate, and one individual or group saying it is does not make it so. In fact, this almost always means that it is not!

Confederate Third National Flag.

The Confederate Flag is also frequently called "controversial" by Liberals. Not because it is, but because they want you to think it is. Pretending the South's "Starry Cross" is controversial, hateful, and racist tends to intimidate, which is the reason this ploy is used by progressives: they cannot tolerate views that contradict their own, so they try to shut down dialog and hamper free speech in an attempt to silence their opponents and critics.

The essential problem here is that hate groups who use the Confederate Flag as a symbol of white supremacy have been misled by the same false mainstream version of Civil War history that Liberals and uneducated Conservatives embrace. They have read and accepted the same anti-South propaganda—namely that "the Confederacy was built on white racism"—and so both have come to believe and accept it, even though they are from opposite ends of the political spectrum.

The true meaning of something is objective; that is, it is beyond opinion, emotion, hearsay, mythology, and political demagoguery. Which brings us to the real question: it is obvious to any intelligent person that the Confederate Battle Flag means something different to different people, but cutting through all of the personal subjectivity, what does it really stand for?

To answer this question we must examine its original, and only true, meaning.

While today the Confederate Battle Flag proudly serves as a wholesome symbol of Southern history, culture, and heritage, originally, as a Christian banner

Confederate soldiers and flags.

representing the armies of a Christian republic fighting for *all* of its people, it first stood for the principles of freedom, personal liberty, states' rights, the Constitution, and Americanism, the hallmarks of every genuine American patriot. It was, in other words, originally a *conservative* emblem of a *conservative* people fighting for *conservative* ideals. The Confederacy was, in fact, the Victorian South's version of today's Republican Party, the Conservative 19th-Century ancestors of modern day conservatism.

In essence then, as the next entry illustrates, the Confederate Battle Flag has nothing to do with racism, and actually represents the polar opposite: its Christian cross is the symbol of the church of the Prince of Peace, whose teaching on universal love and tolerance has been preached from every pulpit in the South for centuries, and still is: "A new commandment I give unto you, that you love one another; as I have loved you, that you also love one another."[429]

Jesus of Nazareth.

Traditional Southerners believe that, as the Bible teaches, there is only one race, and that is the human race. For God "has made from one blood every nation of men to dwell on all the face of the earth."[430] If the Left-wing enemies of the South would only live by the Christian Manifesto as earnestly as they do the Communist Manifesto.

TRUE OR FALSE: Only whites fought under the Confederate Flag.
ANSWER: False. Southern society has always been multiracial and multicultural, and the Rebel military, which was comprised of every race and dozens of different nationalities, reflected this. Thanks to the barbarous Yankee custom of burning down Southern courthouses,[431] exact statistics are impossible to come by. But Southern historians have determined that the following numbers are quite accurate. In descending numerical order the Confederate army and navy were composed of about

- 1 million European-Americans.[432]
- 300,000 to 1 million African-Americans.[433]
- 70,000 Native-Americans.[434]
- 60,000 Latin-Americans.[435]
- 50,000 foreigners.[436]
- 12,000 Jewish-Americans.[437]
- 10,000 Asian-Americans.[438]

True Southerners, of all races, continue to be proud of our region's multiracial history, and of the many contributions made to Dixie and the Southern Cause by individuals of all colors, creeds, and nationalities.[439]

MULTIPLE CHOICE: When is the Confederate Flag coming down?
A. When pigs fly.
B. When Hell freezes over.
C. When the Sun rises in the West.
D. On the twelfth of never.
ANSWER: All of the above.[440]

White and black Confederate soldiers: Andrew M. Chandler (left), Silas Chandler (right), of the 44th Mississippi Infantry.

SIXTEEN

RECONSTRUCTION

MULTIPLE CHOICE: The North's real—that is, secret—purpose behind Reconstruction was

A. to help rebuild the prostrate South after the War.

B. to assist Southerners in reclaiming their shattered lives.

C. to aid in the process of bringing the seceded states back into the Union.

D. the complete deconstruction of every facet of Southern society.

ANSWER: D.[441]

Abraham Lincoln.

QUESTION: What reason did Lincoln give for wanting to reconstruct the South after the War?

ANSWER: Lincoln answered this question when, during a private conversation in 1862, he told Interior Department official T. J. Barnett that the primary object of his War was the "subjugation" of the South, and that the entire region would need to be obliterated and replaced with new businessmen and new ideas.[442] From this it is plain that long before the end of the conflict, Northern Liberals were already committed to the total cultural genocide of the patriotic South. This meant not just the extermination of her Southernness, but the complete liberalization of her conservative citizenry as well.

To Left-wing Yankees then, "reconstruction" did not mean "aid in rebuilding the war-torn South," as our mainstream history books falsely teach, but rather the full-scale Northernization of the 13 seceded Southern states, using whatever physical force and unconstitutional acts were deemed necessary.

Lincoln's subjugation-Northernization plans got the full backing of the majority of his party members (the Republicans, the Liberal party of the day). One of these, the "harsh, cynical, vindictive septuagenarian," Yankee Radical Liberal Thaddeus Stevens, arrogantly called it the "Conquered Province" policy:[443] the entire South was to be confiscated to pay for the costs of the War (that Lincoln started!),[444] and the Confederate states themselves would only be "readmitted" to the Union if they had

Thaddeus Stevens.

been "redeemed"[445]—that is, thoroughly cleansed of their states' rights movements and "rebellious attitudes."[446]

Said Stevens in 1865 before the U.S. House of Representatives: "The whole fabric of southern society must be changed and never can it be done if this opportunity is lost. . . . If the South is ever to be made a safe republic let her lands be cultivated by the toil of the owners or the free labor of intelligent citizens. This must be done even though it drive her nobility into exile. If they go, all the better."[447]

Clearly, the North's "reconstruction" plans had nothing to do with true reconstruction. The word was merely Liberal-speak for a second Civil War on the South, the first one directed at her physical destruction, the second one, "Reconstruction," concerned with cultural, social, emotional, and psychological destruction.[448]

TRUE OR FALSE: Reconstruction was a successful and necessary program to help rebuild the belligerent South and reestablish peaceful relations between the two regions.

ANSWER: False. Like the term the "Civil War," the term "Reconstruction" is one of the greatest misnomers of all time, for no true rebuilding of the Southern states was intended, and indeed none ever took place during the Reconstruction years, 1865 to 1877.

What *did* take place was an attempt at the deconstruction of the Old South and its replacement by the "New South," for one of Lincoln's stated goals was always to Northernize the South and recreate it in the image of the North. This was to occur primarily through massive industrialization and the wholesale takeover of homes, plantations, towns, and businesses by Yankee investors, and more perniciously, the takeover of Southern schools by Yankee teachers.[449]

Since, naturally, the agrarian South would not go down this road willingly, she had to be coerced, which is exactly what the North proceeded to do the very day Lee laid down arms at Appomattox.

But turning the South into a military state under the rule of despotic and often corrupt, arrogant, and violent Yankee officers, did nothing to engender warm feelings toward the North.[450] At the same time, in an

Rutherford B. Hayes.

attempt to thoroughly "Unionize" Southerners,[451] Confederate flags and uniforms were banned,[452] former Confederate officers were required to pay exorbitant taxes and barred from holding political office,[453] and former white Confederates were prohibited from voting while illiterate blacks were given the franchise.[454]

Worse, the North's Reconstruction soldiers often harassed Dixie's citizens, ousted her families from their farms, pillaged their homes, robbed their men, and raped their women.[455] Sadistically, many Southerners were even put on racks and tortured with thumbscrews.[456] Why? What could possibly justify such acts? Only the Yankees who committed these crimes know the answer.

Southerners responded to the violent insanity of carpetbag-scallywag rule just as they did to the North's first illegal invasion of their homeland in 1861: they "rebelled" a second time, and with the help of a new and more enlightened president, Rutherford B. Hayes, by 1877 they were able to drive the last hated Yankee soldiers out of the South.

Free at last from the iron fist of Yankee dictatorship, Southern families returned to their homes and reopened their shops and schools (what was left of them). Former Confederate officers were quickly voted into office and the Confederate Flag was proudly flown once again outside every house, farm, and storefront. With Dixie now in tatters, Southerners did their level best to pick up where they had left off before

Lincoln's illegal invasion sixteen years earlier.

In the end, like the "Civil War" itself, Reconstruction was an utter failure, doomed by the impossibility of its very mission: to make the leisurely, religious, agricultural South into an exact duplicate of the fast-paced, atheistic, industrialized North. It was indeed, as Yankee Albion W. Tourgee noted in 1883, "a fool's errand."[457]

Unfortunately, Lincoln's left-wing liberal dream (to Northernize the South) is still very much alive. Now aided by thousands of disloyal "New South" fools known as scallywags, the sinister process to eliminate all Southernness from Dixie continues, stronger now than ever before. At every opportunity true Southerners continue to resist the trend to exterminate Southern society.[458]

White House of the Confederacy, Richmond, Virginia.

SEVENTEEN

REVIEW OF

HIGHLIGHTS

Jefferson Davis.

TRUE OR FALSE: Abraham Lincoln's Republican Party, the Liberal party in the mid 19th Century, has no connection to today's Republican Party.
ANSWER: True. Today the Civil War era Republican Party is the Democratic Party.[459]

TRUE OR FALSE: Jefferson Davis' Democratic Party, the Conservative party in the mid 19th Century, has no connection to today's Democratic Party.
ANSWER: True. Today the Civil War era Democratic Party is the Republican Party.[460]

QUESTION: Who were the "good guys" in the American Civil War?
ANSWER: If you are a Conservative it was the Confederacy. If you are a Liberal it was the Union.[461]

QUESTION: Who were the "bad guys" in the American Civil War?
ANSWER: If you are a Conservative it was the Union. If you are a Liberal it was the Confederacy.[462]

QUESTION: If the War was not fought over slavery, what was it fought over?
ANSWER: In essence the North was fighting to overthrow the

Constitution, enlarge the federal government, and destroy states' rights; the South was fighting to preserve the Constitution, shrink the federal government, and protect states' rights.[463]

TRUE OR FALSE: The original KKK, the one that formed right after the Civil War, was a racist organization.
ANSWER: False. What I call the Reconstruction Ku Klux Klan was a Conservative organization that was intentionally formed as a *temporary* protective aid and welfare society—which is why it only lasted for a little over three years (1865-1869). During that time it assisted all races.[464]

TRUE OR FALSE: The Civil War KKK and the modern KKK are identical.
ANSWER: False. Other than the name and clothing, the two have no connection, for they have completely different purposes and missions.[465]

TRUE OR FALSE: Both the American slave trade and American slavery started in the North.
ANSWER: True. In Massachusetts to be exact.[466]

TRUE OR FALSE: The American abolition movement was born in the South.
ANSWER: True. In Virginia to be exact.[467]

QUESTION: Why did the South invent the name "The Confederate States of America" in 1861?
ANSWER: The name "The Confederate States of America" was not invented by the Southern states in 1861. It was one of the names originally used for The United States of America, which is why the South borrowed and adopted it as the name of their new confederate republic. This proves that the seceding Southern states were not trying to "takeover" or "destroy" the U.S. government, as mainstream historians teach. By seceding they hoped to preserve the original government of the Founding Fathers, which they referred to as "our confederacy."[468]

"Our government, conceived in freedom and purchased with blood, can be preserved only by constant vigilance. May we guard it as our children's richest legacy, for what shall it profit our nation if it shall gain the whole world and lost 'the spirit that prizes liberty as the heritage of all men in all lands everywhere?'"[469]

WILLIAM JENNINGS BRYAN
The Price of the Soul, 1909

NOTES

1. Woods, p. 47.
2. On Lincoln's socialistic, Marxist, and communist thoughts, ideas, and tendencies, see e.g., McCarty, passim; Browder, passim; Benson and Kennedy, passim.
3. See J. W. Jones, TDMV, pp. 144, 200-201, 273.
4. See Seabrook, TAHSR, passim. See also, Pollard, LC, p. 178; J. H. Franklin, pp. 101, 111, 130, 149; Nicolay and Hay, ALCW, Vol. 1, p. 627.
5. See e.g., Seabrook, TQJD, pp. 30, 38, 76.
6. See e.g., J. Davis, RFCG, Vol. 1, pp. 55, 422; Vol. 2, pp. 4, 161, 454, 610. Besides using the term "Civil War" himself, President Davis cites numerous other individuals who use it as well.
7. See e.g., *Confederate Veteran*, March 1912, Vol. 20, No. 3, p. 122.
8. Minutes of the Eighth Annual Meeting, July 1898, p. 87.
9. I cover this topic in detail in my book *Abraham Lincoln Was a Liberal, Jefferson Davis Was a Conservative: The Missing Key to Understanding the American Civil War.*
10. Seabrook, AWAITBLA, p. 23.
11. Mish, s.v. "secession."
12. Traupman, s.v. "secedo."
13. Mish, s.v. "secession."
14. Seabrook, AWAITBLA, p. 21.
15. Seabrook, AWAITBLA, p. 23.
16. Rawle, p. 290.
17. Seabrook, C101, p. 60.
18. Rawle, pp. 289, 290.
19. Stephens, ACV, Vol. 1, p. 514.
20. Jensen, NN, p. 25; Lancaster and Plumb, p. 197.
21. F. Moore, AE, Vol. 2, p. 204.
22. Seabrook, TQJD, p. 40.
23. Seabrook, AWAITBLA, p. 88.
24. Pollard, LC, p. 96.
25. Seabrook, AWAITBLA, p. 36.
26. Seabrook, C101, pp. 47-49.
27. C. Johnson, pp. 115-117.
28. DeGregorio, s.v. "John Adams" (p. 28).
29. Bledsoe, pp. 137, 138-139, 140.
30. Seabrook, AWAITBLA, p. 70.
31. See Seabrook, LW, passim.
32. Hamilton, Madison, and Jay, p. 21.
33. Foley, pp. 212, 797.
34. Collier and Collier, p. 4.
35. See Seabrook, AWAITBLA, passim.
36. F. Moore, Vol. 7, p. 306.
37. Nicolay and Hay, ALCW, Vol. 2, p. 55.
38. Nicolay and Hay, ALCW, Vol. 2, p. 61.
39. Seabrook, C101, p. 55.
40. Fowler, pp. 249-251.
41. Legal scholars, including the members of the National Constitution Center, consider the Bill of Rights to be "a part of the Constitution."
42. Bledsoe, p. 131.

43. Calvert, Vol. 8, pp. 1-5.

44. Greeley, HSSER, p. 17.

45. Hacker, p. 339.

46. Seabrook, AWAITBLA, pp. 118, 188-190.

47. Seabrook, AWAITBLA, p. 253.

48. Why then does the U.S. Pledge of Allegiance refer to "one *nation*"? Because the Pledge was written by a Yankee socialist, Francis Bellamy of New York. Seabrook, EYWTATCWIW, p. 72.

49. Fowler, p. 249.

50. Seabrook, ALWAL, pp. 109-112.

51. Beach, Vol. 3, s.v. "Calhoun, John Caldwell."

52. It was America's antipathy toward democracy that prompted English novelist Rudyard Kipling to criticize the U.S.A. in the late 1800s. R. Miller, p. 173.

53. Rozwenc, pp. 10-11.

54. Seabrook, AL, p. 42. The U.S. is a *representative democracy* in the sense that we the people elect officials who represent and serve us in Washington, D.C. But this is not the same as a pure democracy.

55. Beach, Vol. 3, s.v. "Calhoun, John Caldwell."

56. Seabrook, C101, passim.

57. Rawle, pp. 9, 93, 296-297.

58. Sage, p. 73.

59. Seabrook, AL, p. 90.

60. Tocqueville, Vol. 2, p. 426.

61. Fowler, p. 217.

62. Seabrook, TAOCE, p. 15.

63. Sage, Appendix I, p. 1.

64. Seabrook, AWAITBLA, pp. 24-25.

65. Rawle, p. 290.

66. Stephens, ACV, Vol. 1, p. 497.

67. Seabrook, EYWTATCWIW, pp. 33-37.

68. Thompson and Wainwright, Vol. 1, p. 44.

69. Ashe, p. 56.

70. Katcher, CWSB, p. 46.

71. Seabrook, EYWTATCWIW, p. 29.

72. Mish, s.v. "civil war."

73. Seabrook, EYWTATCWIW, pp. 23-25.

74. Seabrook, AWAITBLA, pp. 244-268.

75. See Seabrook, LW, passim.

76. See Seabrook, ALWALJDWAC, passim.

77. See Seabrook, LW, passim.

78. Seabrook, TQJD, p. 106.

79. Seabrook, EYWTATCWIW, p. 29.

80. Seabrook, EYWTATCWIW, pp. 30-32.

81. Seabrook, LW, pp. 304-305.

82. See Seabrook, LW, passim.

83. Seabrook, AWAITBLA, pp. 32-33.

84. Seabrook, EYWTATCWIW, p. 109.

85. Seabrook, AWAITBLA, pp. 32-33. While Jefferson "sketched" out the Kentucky Resolutions, James Madison wrote the Virginia Resolutions.

86. Seabrook, AWAITBLA, passim.

87. Seabrook, EYWTATCWIW, pp. 109-110.

88. C. Adams, p. 186; Sobel, s.v. "Davis, Jefferson." Also hoping to prove that secession was legal, numerous other Confederates demanded that they be tried for "treason" by the U.S. government. All were turned down—for obvious reasons. C. Johnson, p. 201.

89. See Seabrook, TGYC, passim.

90. Seabrook, AWAITBLA, p. 347.

91. See Seabrook, AL, passim.
92. Seabrook, EYWTATCWIW, p. 112.
93. C. Johnson, pp. 187-188.
94. J. Davis, RFCG, Vol. 2, p. 701.
95. Hinkle, p. 108.
96. Seabrook, EYWTATCWIW, p. 112.
97. J. Davis, RFCG, Vol. 2, p. 701.
98. Shenkman and Reiger, p. 124.
99. J. Davis, RFCG, Vol. 1, p. 518.
100. Seabrook, EYWTATCWIW, p. 112.
101. Seabrook, LW, pp. 121, 297.
102. Seabrook, S101, p. 67.
103. Seabrook, TGYC, pp. 147-148; Seabrook, EYWTAASIW, pp. 260-264.
104. Seabrook, TQAHS, pp. 16-24.
105. Seabrook, TGYC, p. 92.
106. Seabrook, TQAHS, pp. 16-24.
107. Parry, s.v. "Benjamin, Judah Philip."
108. Neilson, s.v. "Benjamin, Judah Philip."
109. Seabrook, L, p. 24.
110. Seabrook, AWAITBLA, p. 274.
111. Seabrook, EYWTATCWIW, p. 197.
112. Hinkle, p. 108.
113. C. Johnson, p. 5.
114. Seabrook, EYWTATCWIW, pp. 125-127.
115. Seabrook, EYWTAASIW, p. 575.
116. Seabrook, LW, p. 308.
117. Seabrook, EYWTAASIW, p. 783.
118. See Seabrook, AL, passim.
119. See e.g., Oates, AL, p. 17.
120. See e.g., Tagg, passim.
121. Seabrook, TGI, p. 36.
122. See Seabrook, ALWALJDWAC, passim.
123. See Seabrook, AL, passim.
124. Rawle, pp. 9, 93, 296-297.
125. Foley, pp. 212, 797.
126. Collier and Collier, p. 4.
127. Fowler, pp. 249-251.
128. Seabrook, CFF, pp. 16, 37, 317.
129. Seabrook, AL, p. 455.
130. Seabrook, AL, p. 316.
131. Seabrook, EYWTATCWIW, p. 79.
132. Seabrook, AL, pp. 468, 549.
133. Seabrook, TGYC, pp. 190-192.
134. Seabrook, EYWTATCWIW, p. 71.
135. Quarles, p. 68.
136. Seabrook, AL, p. 248.
137. C. Adams, p. 135; DiLorenzo, GC, p. 255; Johannsen, p. 55.
138. Seabrook, AL, p. 479, passim.
139. Seabrook, LW, p. 29.
140. Seabrook, TUAL, p. 91.
141. Seabrook, ALWALJDWAC, pp. 77-79.
142. Seabrook, LW, pp. 28-29.
143. Seabrook, AL, pp. 132-133.
144. Seabrook, TGYC, pp. 173-174.

145. Seabrook, AL, p. 257.
146. Seabrook, TGYC, p. 174.
147. Seabrook, AL, p. 264; Seabrook, EYWTAASIW, pp. 124-125.
148. Minutes of the Ninth Annual Meeting, May 1899, pp. 200-201.
149. Seabrook, EYWTATCWIW, p. 145.
150. See Seabrook, AWAITBLA, passim.
151. Seabrook, EYWTATCWIW, pp. 29-30.
152. Seabrook, AWAITBLA, p. 144.
153. Seabrook, AWAITBLA, pp. 145-146.
154. Munford, p. 167.
155. Seabrook, AWAITBLA, p. 317.
156. Seabrook, LW, p. 169.
157. Seabrook, TQREL, p. 226.
158. Seabrook, TQREL, p. 110.
159. See Seabrook, AWAITBLA, passim.
160. Seabrook, TQREL, passim.
161. Seabrook, TQREL, p. 213.
162. Seabrook, ARB, p. 11.
163. Seabrook, AWAITBLA, p. 165.
164. Seabrook, AWAITBLA, pp. 137-138.
165. Seabrook, EYWTATCWIW, p. 90.
166. Seabrook, AL, pp. 179-180.
167. For Forrest's full true life story, see Seabrook, ARB, passim.
168. See Seabrook, EYWTATCWIW, passim; TGYC, passim; LW, passim.
169. Seabrook, ARB, p. 152.
170. Seabrook, ARB, p. 259.
171. Seabrook, ARB, p. 144.
172. Seabrook, ARB, p. 263.
173. Seabrook, ARB, pp. 459-460.
174. Seabrook, TQSJ, pp. 14, 27.
175. Seabrook, TQSJ, pp. 19, 372-374.
176. Seabrook, EYWTATCWIW, p. 87.
177. See Seabrook, EYWTAASIW, passim.
178. Seabrook, TQSJ, p. 374.
179. Seabrook, TQSJ, p. 17.
180. Seabrook, LW, p. 51.
181. Seabrook, EYWTAASIW, p. 180.
182. Seabrook, ARB, pp. 275-276.
183. Seabrook, ARB, p. 276.
184. U. S. Grant, Vol. 1, p. 327.
185. Seabrook, ARB, p. 276.
186. Seabrook, ARB, p. 276.
187. Seabrook, S101, pp. 74-79.
188. Seabrook, TGYC, p. 142.
189. Seabrook, TGYC, p. 142.
190. Seabrook, TGYC, p. 142.
191. Seabrook, TGYC, pp. 142-143.
192. Seabrook, TGYC, p. 143.
193. Seabrook, AL, p. 317.
194. Seabrook, TGYC, p. 143.
195. Seabrook, AL, p. 437.
196. Seabrook, AL, p. 437.
197. Seabrook, AL, p. 436.
198. Napolitano, p. 73.

199. Gragg, pp. 177-181.

200. J. Davis, RFCG, Vol. 2, p. 634.

201. Hurmence, pp. 99-102; J. Davis, RFCG, Vol. 2, p. 716.

202. Gragg, pp. 182-183, 188.

203. Stonebraker, pp. 170-171.

204. ORA, Ser. 1, Vol. 39, Pt. 3, p. 494.

205. Seabrook, EYWTATCWIW, p. 185.

206. ORA, Ser. 1, Vol. 39, Pt. 2, p. 132.

207. Flood, p. 400; Kennett, p. 107; C. Johnson, p. 167.

208. Seabrook, EYWTATCWIW, p. 182.

209. Seabrook, EYWTATCWIW, pp. 182-184.

210. Seabrook, EYWTATCWIW, pp. 117, 124; Seabrook, LW, pp. 75, 229; Seabrook, ALWALJDWAC, p. 80; Benson and Kennedy, p. 143.

211. Seabrook, AL, pp. 377-378; Seabrook, EYWTATCWIW, p. 171.

212. Seabrook, AL, p. 190.

213. See Chesnut, ADFD, passim; Chesnut, MCCW, passim.

214. Seabrook, WIG, p. 259.

215. See Nicolay and Hay, CWAL, Vol. 11, pp. 105-106; Nicolay and Hay, ALCW, Vol. 1, p. 483; Holzer, pp. 22-23, 67, 318, 361.

216. W. S. Kennedy, pp. 34-35.

217. Seabrook, AL, pp. 241-260.

218. Nicolay and Hay, ALCW, Vol. 1, p. 292.

219. Seabrook, WIG, p. 95.

220. See Seabrook, EOTBOF, passim.

221. Seabrook, TMOCP, pp. 506-507.

222. Seabrook, CPGS, p. 24.

223. Bradley, pp. 45-46.

224. Seabrook, EYWTATCWIW, pp. 182-184.

225. Seabrook, EYWTATCWIW, pp. 82-83.

226. Seabrook, ARB, pp. 234-235.

227. Seabrook, TGYC, pp. 92-94.

228. Seabrook, TGYC, p. 131.

229. J. M. McPherson, BCOF, p. 138. For more on Greeley and socialism see Sotheran, passim.

230. Benson and Kennedy, p. 71.

231. Seabrook, LW, p. 74.

232. Seabrook, ALWALJDWAC, pp. 77-79.

233. See Seabrook, ALWALJDWAC, passim.

234. Seabrook, LW, passim.

235. Seabrook, AL, p. 197.

236. Seabrook, EYWTAASIW, pp. 547-645.

237. Seabrook, LW, p. 56.

238. Seabrook, AL, p. 190. For more on the cause of Lincoln's War, see Seabrook, LW, passim.

239. Seabrook, AL, p. 190; Seabrook, LW, pp. 77-78.

240. Nicolay and Hay, ALCW, Vol. 1, p. 609.

241. J. M. McPherson, BCOF, p. 205.

242. Seabrook, ARB, p. 48.

243. Seabrook, EYWTATCWIW, p. 139.

244. Seabrook, AL, pp. 30, 147.

245. Seabrook, LW, passim.

246. Seabrook, TGYC, p. 50.

247. For more on this topic, see Seabrook, EYWTAASIW, pp 595-623.

248. See Seabrook, AWAITBLA, pp. 144, 166-167, 310.

249. Ashe, p. 39.

250. Barney, p. 124. Instead, Douglass and many other Northern blacks supported Gerrit Smith that year, the presidential candidate of the Radical abolitionist party.

251. *Douglass' Monthly*, September, 1861, Vol. 4, p. 516.

252. *Douglass' Monthly*, September 1862, Vol. 5, pp. 707-708.

253. Seabrook, EYWTAASIW, pp. 732, 745-746, 769-771.

254. Seabrook, ALWALJDWAC, pp. 79, 83-84.

255. See DiLorenzo, LU, p. 101.

256. Seabrook, TUAL, pp. 90-107.

257. Douglass, LTFD, p. 872.

258. Sotheran, p. 192.

259. R. W. Emerson, JRWE, Vol. 4, pp. 312-313.

260. Seabrook, AL, p. 190.

261. For more on biblical figures and slavery, see Seabrook, EYWTAASIW, pp. 400-419.

262. Seabrook, AL, pp. 113-114, 458-459.

263. Seabrook, AL, p. 268.

264. Seabrook, ARB, p. 106; Seabrook, AL, pp. 88, 550; Fogel, p. 254; Greeley, AC, Vol. 2, p. 524; Murphy, p. 86; Cooper, JDA, p. 610; J. M. McPherson, BCOF, p. 138; Benson and Kennedy, p. 71; Seabrook, LW, pp. 256-257; Snay, p. 56; Seabrook, ALWALJDWAC, pp. 139-140.

265. Seabrook, AL, pp. 499-503; Lamon, LAL, p. 489; Christian, p. 10.

266. Seabrook, AL, p. 258.

267. C. Johnson, pp. 187-188.

268. Seabrook, LW, p. 73; Seabrook, L, pp. 113-114.

269. Seabrook, LW, p. 94.

270. Lincoln leaned toward democratic socialism, Hitler was a national socialist. Seabrook, LW, p. 95.

271. For a discussion on Lincoln and Hitler, as well as a list of their similarities, see Seabrook, CFF, pp. 287-294.

272. Seabrook, TUAL, p. 81.

273. As just one example, the town of Americana, Brazil, is still a major center of Confederate loyalty.

274. Seabrook, EYWTATCWIW, p. 205.

275. Seabrook, AL, pp. 76-77.

276. Seabrook, LW, p. 74.

277. See Seabrook, AL, pp. 263-292.

278. Tourgee, p. 300.

279. Greenberg and Waugh, pp. 351-358.

280. Seabrook, AL, pp. 241-260.

281. McKissack and McKissack, pp. 138-139.

282. Seabrook, AL, p. 341.

283. Seabrook, AL, p. 204.

284. The names of the individuals killed by Turner and his men on August 21 and 22, 1831, are as follows: Joseph Travers and wife and three children; Mrs. Elizabeth Turner; Hartwell Prebles; Sarah Newsome; Mrs. P. Reese and son William; Trajan Doyle; Henry Bryant and wife and child, and wife's mother; Mrs. Catherine Whitehead, son Richard and four daughters and grandchild; Salathiel Francis; Nathaniel Francis' overseer and two children; John T. Barrow; George Vaughan; Mrs. Levi Waller and ten children; William Williams, wife and two boys; Mrs. Caswell Worrell and child; Mrs. Rebecca Vaughan; Ann Eliza Vaughan, and son Arthur; Mrs. John K. Williams and child; Mrs. Jacob Williams and three children; Edwin Drury.

285. For the complete and *true* story of the Nat Turner rebellion, see T. R. Gray, passim.

286. Though a psychopathic murderer and an overt racist, strangely, Turner continues to be regarded as a romantic and political hero by many blacks around the world. His end was not very heroic, however. After his short but violent life came to a close at the end of the hangman's noose, he was skinned, beheaded, and quartered, his body parts handed out as gruesome souvenirs. Dozens of lives were lost, including Turner's. For what? His death, by strengthening the very institution he was trying to destroy, helped postpone emancipation for decades and turned thousands of white Southern abolitionists into pro-slavery advocates and Negrophobes. Slavery was coming to a natural end. Unfortunately, like Lincoln thirty years later, Turner showed no interest in abolishing slavery peacefully through the use of compensated manumission, as most other nations around the world had done, or were considering at the time. Instead, both men chose the path

of violence, living and dying by the sword, acts that left wounds in the American psyche that will never heal.
287. Seabrook, TAOCE, p. 11.
288. For an in-depth discussion of the development of the U.S., see Seabrook, C101, passim.
289. Website: www.usa.gov/federal-agencies/a.
290. J. H. Moore, p. 163.
291. Bryan, LAS, p. 279.
292. Faulkner, p. 136.
293. Rutherford, TOH, p. 28.
294. Rutherford, TOH, p. ix.
295. J. G. Randall, p. 79.
296. Seabrook, AL, pp. 27, 68.
297. Macy, p. 247; Faulkner, p. 346; F. Curtis, Vol. 1, p. 271.
298. Seabrook, AL, pp. 67-68.
299. Seabrook, ALWALJDWAC, pp. 89-90.
300. Seabrook, ALWALJDWAC, passim; Seabrook, LW, passim.
301. Seabrook, AWAITBLA, p. 31; Seabrook, CFF, pp. 24, 278-284, 303; Seabrook, p. 183. See also Muzzey, Vol. 1, p. 521.
302. Seabrook, C101, p. 13.
303. Seabrook, TGYC, pp. 27-30.
304. Seabrook, C101, pp. 21, 32-38.
305. Seabrook, C101, pp. 39-40.
306. Seabrook, C101, pp. 75-76.
307. See Seabrook, C101, passim; Seabrook, TAOCE, passim; Seabrook, TCOTCSOAE, passim.
308. Seabrook, C101, p. 93.
309. Seabrook, TGYC, pp. 29-30.
310. Sage, p. 73.
311. Rozwenc, pp. 10-11.
312. See Seabrook, AWAITBLA, passim.
313. Collier and Collier, p. 4.
314. Foley, pp. 212, 797.
315. Hamilton, Madison, and Jay, p. 21.
316. Sage, p. 90. Emphasis added.
317. The word "federal" is a shortening, abbreviation, or corruption of the word "confederal," which means "confederacy." See Seabrook, AL, pp. 15-21.
318. Stephens, ACV, Vol. 1, p. 503.
319. Sage, pp. 104-105. Emphasis added.
320. See Benson and Kennedy, pp. 51-73, 285.
321. Seabrook, LW, p. 76.
322. Seabrook, EYWTAASIW, pp. 55-61.
323. Seabrook, EYWTAASIW, pp. 3, 62-119.
324. Seabrook, EYWTATCWIW, p. 75.
325. Seabrook, TGYC, p. 91.
326. Seabrook, EYWTATCWIW, pp. 69-98.
327. Seabrook, TGYC, pp. 111-112.
328. Seabrook, EYWTAASIW, pp. 215-216.
329. Seabrook, TGYC, p. 113.
330. Seabrook, AL, p. 170.
331. Seabrook, EYWTAASIW, p. 420.
332. Seabrook, EYWTATCWIW, p. 89.
333. Seabrook, TGYC, p. 115.
334. See Seabrook, EYWTAASIW, passim.
335. Stampp, p. 192.
336. Fogel and Engerman, pp. 151-152, 241; M. M. Smith, pp. 184-185.
337. Fogel, p. 194.

338. Seabrook, EYWTATCWIW, pp. 79-81.

339. Seabrook, EYWTATCWIW, p. 80.

340. See Seabrook, EYWTAASIW, passim.

341. Seabrook, EYWTAASIW, pp. 28, 129-131, 137, 155-163.

342. Seabrook, EYWTAASIW, pp. 57-59, 248-250.

343. For more on white slavery in early America, see Baepler, passim; Ballagh, passim; Galenson, passim; Hildreth, passim; Hoffman, passim; Jordan and Walsh, passim.

344. C. Johnson, pp. 81-84.

345. Seabrook, EYWTAASIW, p. 245.

346. Seabrook, EYWTAASIW, p. 246.

347. Seabrook, EYWTAASIW, p. 441.

348. Seabrook, EYWTAASIW, pp. 441-443.

349. See Seabrook, EYWTAASIW, pp. 459-513.

350. Seabrook, EYWTAASIW, p. 459.

351. Seabrook, EYWTAASIW, pp. 459-460.

352. Seabrook, EYWTAASIW, pp. 430-432.

353. Seabrook, EYWTAASIW, pp. 197, 432-433.

354. Seabrook, EYWTAASIW, p. 549.

355. Seabrook, EYWTAASIW, pp. 553, 554-569.

356. Seabrook, EYWTAASIW, pp. 566-567.

357. Seabrook, EYWTAASIW, p. 571.

358. Seabrook, EYWTAASIW, pp. 599-602, 736.

359. Seabrook, EYWTAASIW, pp. 601-602.

360. Seabrook, EYWTATCWIW, pp. 104-108.

361. Seabrook, AWAITBLA, pp. 149, 268, 275.

362. Seabrook, TGYC, pp. 190-192.

363. Seabrook, AL, p. 565.

364. Seabrook, AL, pp. 225, 237, 242-243, 250, 479.

365. Seabrook, AL, pp. 371-410.

366. See my book of the same name.

367. Seabrook, EYWTAASIW, p. 557.

368. Seabrook, EYWTAASIW, pp. 242-243.

369. Buckingham, Vol. 2, p. 112.

370. Tocqueville, Vol. 1, p. 383.

371. Seabrook, EYWTAASIW, pp. 679-684.

372. Seabrook, AL, p. 252.

373. Flood, p. 400; Kennett, p. 107; C. Johnson, p. 167.

374. Seabrook, TUAL, pp. 81, 91.

375. U.S. gov. Website: www.nps.gov/gett/forteachers/upload/7%20Lincoln%20on%20Race.pdf.

376. Seabrook, NBFATKKK, p. 32.

377. Seabrook, ARB, pp. 459-460.

378. Seabrook, ARB, p. 12.

379. Seabrook, EYWTATCWIW, p. 172.

380. Seabrook, EYWTATCWIW, p. 172.

381. Seabrook, S101, p. 40; Seabrook, EYWTAASIW, p. 86.

382. Seabrook, S101, p. 40.

383. For more on "The Great Yankee Coverup," see my book of the same name.

384. Seabrook, TQJD, p. 94.

385. Livermore, pp. 4, 7.

386. W. B. Garrison, CWT, p. 153.

387. Katcher, CWSB, p. 120. Also see *The Civil War Book of Lists*, p. 95.

388. Seabrook, EYWTATCWIW, pp. 188-190.

389. Current, TC, s.v. "Prisons."

390. DiLorenzo, RL, pp. 140-141.

391. W. B. Garrison, CWT, p. 160.

392. Seabrook, EYWTATCWIW, pp. 189-190.

393. Whitman, p. 125.

394. Seabrook, EYWTATCWIW, pp. 191-192.

395. Boatner, s.v. "Trent Affair."

396. Seabrook, EYWTATCWIW, pp. 193-194.

397. Seabrook, EYWTAASIW, pp. 420-444.

398. Owsley, pp. 65-66, 187-190.

399. E. M. Thomas, pp. 293-294.

400. J. D. Richardson, Vol. 2, pp. 709, 713; Owsley, pp. 538-541; Durden, pp. 149-150; Cooper, JDA, pp. 552-553.

401. Eaton, HSC, p. 81.

402. Nicolay and Hay, ALCW, Vol. 2, p. 302.

403. Nicolay and Hay, ALCW, Vol. 2, p. 1.

404. See e.g., Nicolay and Hay, ALCW, Vol. 2, pp. 227-228.

405. Seabrook, EYWTATCWIW, pp. 194-195.

406. Seabrook, AWAITBLA, pp. 312-313.

407. See Seabrook, NBFATKKK, passim.

408. Seabrook, NBFATKKK, p. 101.

409. Seabrook, NBFATKKK, pp. 30-32, 56, 58, 80, 87, 89, 98-99.

410. Seabrook, NBFATKKK, pp. 29, 32, 43, 112.

411. Seabrook, TQNBF, p. 105.

412. Seabrook, NBFATKKK, pp. 38-39, 42, 79.

413. Seabrook, NBFATKKK, p. 118.

414. Seabrook, NBFATKKK, pp. 26, 29-32.

415. Seabrook, NBFATKKK, p. 118.

416. Seabrook, NBFATKKK, pp. 36, 42-43.

417. See Seabrook, NBFATKKK, passim.

418. Seabrook, NBFATKKK, p. 101.

419. Seabrook, NBFATKKK, p. 36.

420. Seabrook, NBFATKKK, pp. 14-15, 102, 118.

421. Seabrook, NBFATKKK, pp. 103-104.

422. See Seabrook, NBFATKKK, passim.

423. Seabrook, NBFATKKK, p. 102.

424. See Seabrook, CFF, passim.

425. See Seabrook, LW, passim.

426. Seabrook, AWAITBLA, pp. 350-351.

427. For a complete discussion of secession, see Seabrook, AWAITBLA, passim.

428. Seabrook, CFF, p. 70.

429. John 13:34.

430. Acts 17:24-26.

431. Seabrook, ARB, p. 259.

432. Eaton, HSC, p. 93.

433. Barrow, Segars, and Rosenburg, BC, p. 97; Hinkle, p. 106; *The United Daughters of the Confederacy Magazine*, Vols. 54-55, 1991, p. 32. If we utilize Yankee General August Valentine Kautz's definition of a "soldier" (that is, anyone who receives pay, which puts him under military law), then as many as 1 million Southern blacks served in one capacity or another in the Confederate military. See Kautz, p. 11.

434. Hinkle, p. 108.

435. See Quintero, Gonzales, and Velazquez, passim.

436. Lonn, p. 218.

437. Rosen, p. 161.

438. Hinkle, p. 108; Blackerby, passim.

439. Seabrook, EYWTATCWIW, pp. 196-199; Seabrook, AL, p. 343.

440. For a full discussion of the Confederate Battle Flag and the three National Confederate Flags, see Seabrook, CFF, passim.

441. See Seabrook, AL, pp. 523-547.

442. Seabrook, NBFATKKK, pp. 44, 108; Catton, Vol. 2, p. 443.

443. Muzzey, Vol. 2, p. 5.

444. Chodes, p. 98; P. M. Roberts, p. 226.

445. J. H. Franklin, p. 196.

446. Hacker, p. 589.

447. *"Reconstruction": Speech of the Hon. Thaddeus Stevens*, p. 7. Delivered at Lancaster, Pennsylvania, September 7, 1865.

448. For a detailed discussion of Reconstruction, see Seabrook, AL, pp. 523-547; Seabrook, NBFATKKK, passim.

449. For a full discussion of Lincoln's plans to Northernize the South, see Seabrook, AL, pp. 519-570.

450. J. H. Franklin, p. 40.

451. Simpson, pp. 62-63.

452. Grissom, p. 180.

453. Simpson, p. 62; J. H. Franklin, p. 144.

454. A. Cooke, ACA, p. 219.

455. Horn, IE, pp. 287-288.

456. Horn, IE, pp. 258-260.

457. Tourgee, p. 300.

458. Seabrook, EYWTATCWIW, pp. 200-201.

459. See Seabrook, ALWALJDWAC, passim.

460. See Seabrook, ALWALJDWAC, passim.

461. See Seabrook, LW, passim.

462. See Seabrook, LW, passim.

463. See Seabrook, LW, passim.

464. See Seabrook, NBFATKKK, passim.

465. See Seabrook, NBFATKKK, passim.

466. See Seabrook, EYWTAASIW, passim.

467. See Seabrook, EYWTAASIW, passim.

468. See Seabrook, CFF, passim; Seabrook, C101, passim.

469. Bryan, HTHA, p. 17.

BIBLIOGRAPHY

Note: My pro-South readers are to be advised that the majority of the books listed here are anti-South in nature (some extremely so), and were written primarily by liberal elitist, socialist, communist, and Marxist authors who loathe the South, and typically the United States and the U.S. Constitution as well. Despite this, as a scholar I find these titles indispensable, for *an honest evaluation of Lincoln's War is not possible without studying both the Southern and the Northern versions*—an attitude, unfortunately, completely lacking among pro-North historians (who read and study only their own ahistorical version). Still, it must be said that the material contained in these often mean-spirited works is largely the result of a century and a half of Yankee myth, falsehoods, cherry-picking, slander, sophistry, editorializing, anti-South propaganda, outright lies, and junk research, as modern pro-North writers merely copy one another's errors without ever looking at the original 19th-Century sources. This type of literature, filled as it is with both misinformation and disinformation, is called "scholarly" and "objective" by pro-North advocates. In the process, the mistakes and lies in these fact-free, fault-ridden, South-shaming, historically inaccurate works have been magnified over the years, and the North's version of the "Civil War" has come to be accepted as the only legitimate one. Indeed, it is now the only one known by most people. That over 95 percent of the titles in my bibliography fall into the anti-South category is simply a reflection of the enormous power and influence that the pro-North movement—our nation's cultural ruling class—has long held over America's education system, libraries, publishing houses, and media (paper and electronic). My books serve as a small rampart against the overwhelming tide of anti-South Fascists, Liberals, cultural Marxists, and political elites, all who are working hard to obliterate Southern culture and guarantee that you will never learn the Truth about Lincoln and his War on the Constitution and the American people.

ADAMS, CHARLES. *When in the Course of Human Events: Arguing the Case for Southern Secession.* Lanham, MD: Rowman and Littlefield, 2000.

ADAMS, FRANCIS D., and BARRY SANDERS. *Alienable Rights: The Exclusion of African Americans in a White Man's Land, 1619-2000.* 2003. New York, NY: Perennial, 2004 ed.

ADAMS, HENRY (ed.). *Documents Relating to New-England Federalism, 1800-1815.* Boston, MA: Little, Brown, and Co., 1877.

ADAMS, NEHEMIAH. *A South-side View of Slavery: Three Months at the South, in 1854.* Boston, MA: T. R. Marvin, 1855.

ALEXANDER, WILLIAM T. *History of the Colored Race in America.* Kansas City, MO: Palmetto Publishing, 1887.

ALOTTA, ROBERT I. *Civil War Justice: Union Army Executions Under Lincoln.* Shippensburg, PA: White Mane, 1989.

ASHE, CAPTAIN SAMUEL A'COURT. *A Southern View of the Invasion of the Southern States and War of 1861-1865.* 1935. Crawfordville, GA: Ruffin Flag Co., 1938 ed.

BAEPLER, PAUL (ed.). *White Slaves, African Masters: An Anthology of American Barbary Captivity Narratives.* Chicago, IL: University of Chicago Press, 1999.

BAILEY, ANNE C. *African Voices of the Atlantic Slave Trade: Beyond the Silence and the Shame.* Boston, MA: Beacon Press, 2005.

BAILEY, HUGH C. *Hinton Rowan Helper: Abolitionist-Racist.* Tuscaloosa, AL: University of Alabama Press, 1965.

BALLAGH, JAMES CURTIS. *White Servitude in the Colony of Virginia: A Study of the System of Indentured Servitude in the American Colonies.* Whitefish, MT: Kessinger Publishing, 2004.

BANCROFT, FREDERIC. *The Life of William H. Seward.* 2 vols. New York, NY: Harper and Brothers, 1900.

——. *Slave-Trading in the Old South*. Baltimore, MD: J. H. Furst, 1931.

BANCROFT, FREDERIC, and WILLIAM A. DUNNING (eds.). *The Reminiscences of Carl Schurz*. 3 vols. New York, NY: McClure Co., 1909.

BANKS, NOREEN. *Early American Almanac*. New York, NY: Bantam, 1975.

BARNEY, WILLIAM L. *Flawed Victory: A New Perspective on the Civil War*. New York, NY: Praeger Publishers, 1975.

BATTLE, KEMP PLUMMER. *History of the University of North Carolina: From its Beginning to the Death of President Swain, 1789-1868*. 2 vols. Raleigh, NC: self-published, 1907.

BEACH, FREDERICK CONVERSE (ed.). *The Encyclopedia Americana: A Universal Reference Library*. 16 vols. New York, NY: Scientific American Compiling Co., 1903-1905.

BEECHER, HENRY WARD. *The Life of Jesus the Christ*. New York, NY: J. B. Ford and Co., 1871.

BENSON, AL, JR., and WALTER DONALD KENNEDY. *Lincoln's Marxists*. Gretna, LA: Pelican, 2011.

BLEDSOE, ALBERT TAYLOR. *Is Davis a Traitor; or Was Secession a Constitutional Right Previous to the War of 1861?* Richmond, VA: The Hermitage Press, 1907.

BOATNER, MARK MAYO. *The Civil War Dictionary*. 1959. New York, NY: David McKay Co., 1988 ed.

BOYD, JAMES P. *Parties, Problems, and Leaders of 1896: An Impartial Presentation of Living National Questions*. Chicago, IL: Publishers' Union, 1896.

BRADLEY, MICHAEL R. *Nathan Bedford Forrest's Escort and Staff*. Gretna, LA: Pelican Publishing Co., 2006.

BROWDER, EARL. *Lincoln and the Communists*. New York, NY: Workers Library Publishers, Inc., 1936.

BRYAN, WILLIAM JENNINGS. *The First Battle: A Story of the Campaign of 1896*. Chicago, IL: W. B. Conkey Co., 1896.

——. *Life and Speeches of Hon. Wm. Jennings Bryan*. Baltimore, MD: R. H. Woodward Co., 1900.

——. *Heart to Heart Appeals*. New York, NY: Fleming H. Revell Co., 1917.

BUCKINGHAM, JAMES SILK. *The Slave States of America*. 2 vols. London, UK: Fisher, Son, and Co., 1842.

BURNS, JAMES MACGREGOR. *The Vineyard of Liberty*. New York, NY: Alfred A. Knopf, 1982.

CALVERT, THOMAS H. *The Federal Statutes Annotated*. 10 vols. Northport, NY: Edward Thompson, 1905.

CATTON, BRUCE. *The Coming Fury* (Vol. 1). 1961. New York, NY: Washington Square Press, 1967 ed.

——. *Terrible Swift Sword* (Vol. 2). 1963. New York, NY: Pocket Books, 1967 ed.

——. *A Stillness at Appomattox* (Vol. 3). 1953. New York, NY: Pocket Books, 1966 ed.

CHESNUT, MARY. *A Diary From Dixie: As Written by Mary Boykin Chesnut, Wife of James Chesnut, Jr., United States Senator from South Carolina, 1859-1861, and afterward an Aide to Jefferson Davis and a Brigadier-General in the Confederate Army*. (Isabella D. Martin and Myrta Lockett Avary, eds.). New York, NY: D. Appleton and Co., 1905 ed.

——. *Mary Chesnut's Civil War*. 1860-1865 (Woodward, Comer Vann, ed.). New Haven, CT: Yale University Press, 1981 ed.

CHODES, JOHN. *Destroying the Republic: Jabez Curry and the Re-Education of the Old South*. New York, NY: Algora, 2005.

CHRISTIAN, GEORGE L. *Abraham Lincoln: An Address Delivered Before R. E. Lee Camp, No. 1 Confederate Veterans at Richmond, VA, October 29, 1909*. Richmond, VA: L. H. Jenkins, 1909.

Civil War Book of Lists, The. 1993. Edison, NJ: Castle Books, 2004 ed.

COLLIER, CHRISTOPHER, and JAMES LINCOLN COLLIER. *Decision in Philadelphia: The Constitutional Convention of 1787*. 1986. New York, NY: Ballantine, 1987 ed.

COOKE, ALISTAIR. *Alistair Cooke's America*. 1973. New York, NY: Alfred A. Knopf, 1984 ed.

COOKE, JOHN ESTEN. *A Life of General Robert E. Lee*. New York, NY: D. Appleton and Co., 1871.

COOLEY, HENRY S. *A Study of Slavery in New Jersey*. Baltimore, MD: Johns Hopkins University Press, 1896.

COOPER, WILLIAM J., JR. *Jefferson Davis, American*. New York, NY: Vintage, 2000.

——. (ed.). *Jefferson Davis: The Essential Writings*. New York, NY: Random House, 2003.

CURRENT, RICHARD N. *The Lincoln Nobody Knows*. 1958. New York, NY: Hill and Wang, 1963 ed.

——. (ed.) *The Confederacy (Information Now Encyclopedia)*. 1993. New York, NY: Macmillan, 1998 ed.

CURTI, MERLE, WILLARD THORPE, and CARLOS BAKER (eds.). *American Issues: The Social Record*. 1941. Chicago, IL: J. B. Lippincott, 1960 ed.

CURTIS, FRANCIS. *The Republican Party: A History of Its Fifty Years' Existence and a Record of Its Measures and Leaders, 1854-1904*. 2 vols. New York, NY: G. P. Putnam's Sons, 1904.

CURTIS, GEORGE TICKNOR. *Life of James Buchanan: Fifteenth President of the United States*. 2 vols. New York, NY: Harper and Brothers, 1883.

CURTIS, WILLIAM ELEROY. *Abraham Lincoln*. Philadelphia, PA: J. B. Lippincott Co., 1902.

DABNEY, ROBERT LEWIS. *A Defense of Virginia and the South*. Dahlonega, GA: Confederate Reprint Co., 1999.

DAHL, ROBERT A. *A Preface to Democratic Theory*. Chicago, IL: University of Chicago Press, 1956.

DAVIS, JEFFERSON. *The Rise and Fall of the Confederate Government*. 2 vols. New York, NY: D. Appleton and Co., 1881.

DEGREGORIO, WILLIAM A. *The Complete Book of U.S. Presidents*. 1984. New York, NY: Barricade, 1993 ed.

DILORENZO, THOMAS J. "The Great Centralizer: Abraham Lincoln and the War Between the States." *The Independent Review*, Vol. 3, No. 2, Fall 1998, pp. 243-271.

——. *The Real Lincoln: A New Look at Abraham Lincoln, His Agenda, and an Unnecessary War*. Three Rivers, MI: Three Rivers Press, 2003.

——. *Lincoln Unmasked: What You're Not Supposed to Know About Dishonest Abe*. New York, NY: Crown Forum, 2006.

DOUGLASS, FREDERICK. *Narrative of the Life of Frederick Douglass: An American Slave*. 1845. New York, NY: Signet, 1997 ed.

——. *The Life and Times of Frederick Douglass, From 1817 to 1882*. London, UK: Christian Age Office, 1882.

DURDEN, ROBERT F. *The Gray and the Black: The Confederate Debate on Emancipation*. Baton Rouge, LA: Louisiana State University Press, 1972.

EARLY, JUBAL A. *A Memoir of the Last Year of the War for Independence in the Confederate States of America*. Lynchburg, VA: Charles W. Button, 1867.

EATON, CLEMENT. *A History of the Southern Confederacy*. 1945. New York, NY: Free Press, 1966 ed.

——. *Jefferson Davis*. New York, NY: Free Press, 1977.

EMERSON, RALPH WALDO. *The Complete Works of Ralph Waldo Emerson*. 12 vols. 1878. Boston, MA: Houghton, Mifflin and Co., 1904 ed.

——. *Journals of Ralph Waldo Emerson*. 10 vols. Edward Waldo Emerson and Waldo Emerson Forbes, eds. Boston, MA: Houghton, Mifflin and Co., 1910.

——. *The Journals and Miscellaneous Notebooks of Ralph Waldo Emerson*. 16 vols. Cambridge, MA: Belknap Press, 1975.

FAULKNER, HAROLD UNDERWOOD. *American Political and Social History*. 1937. New York, NY: Appleton-Century-Crofts, 1948 ed.

FITCH, MICHAEL H. *Echoes of the Civil War as I Hear Them*. New York, NY: R. F. Fenno and Co., 1905.

FLOOD, CHARLES BRACELEN. *1864: Lincoln At the Gates of History*. New York, NY: Simon and Schuster, 2009.

FOGEL, ROBERT WILLIAM. *Without Consent or Contract: The Rise and Fall of American Slavery*. New York, NY: W. W. Norton, 1989.

FOGEL, ROBERT WILLIAM, and STANLEY L. ENGERMAN. *Time On the Cross: The Economics of American Negro Slavery*. Boston, MA: Little, Brown, and Co., 1974.

FOLEY, JOHN P. (ed.). *The Jeffersonian Cyclopedia*. New York, NY: Funk and Wagnalls, 1900.

FOWLER, WILLIAM CHAUNCEY. *The Sectional Controversy; or Passages in the Political History of the United States, Including the Causes of the War Between the Sections*. New York, NY: Charles Scribner, 1864.

FRANKLIN, JOHN HOPE. *Reconstruction After the Civil War*. Chicago, IL: University of Chicago Press, 1961.

FURNAS, J. C. *The Americans: A Social History of the United States, 1587-1914*. New York, NY: G. P. Putnam's Sons, 1969.

GALENSON, DAVID W. *White Servitude in Colonial America*. New York, NY: Cambridge University Press, 1981.

GARRISON, WEBB B. *Civil War Trivia and Fact Book*. Nashville, TN: Rutledge Hill Press, 1992.

——. *The Lincoln No One Knows: The Mysterious Man Who Ran the Civil War*. Nashville, TN: Rutledge Hill Press, 1993.

——. *Civil War Curiosities: Strange Stories, Oddities, Events, and Coincidences*. Nashville, TN: Rutledge Hill Press, 1994.

——. *The Amazing Civil War*. Nashville, TN: Rutledge Hill Press, 1998.

GORHAM, GEORGE C. *Life and Public Services of Edwin M. Stanton*. 2 vols. Boston, MA: Houghton, Mifflin and Co., 1899.

GRAGG, ROD. *The Illustrated Confederate Reader: Extraordinary Eyewitness Accounts by the Civil War's Southern Soldiers and Civilians*. New York, NY: Gramercy Books, 1989.

GRANT, ULYSSES SIMPSON. *Personal Memoirs of U. S. Grant*. 2 vols. 1885-1886. New York, NY: Charles L. Webster and Co., 1886.

GRAY, THOMAS R. *The Confessions of Nat Turner: The Leader of the Late Insurrection in Southampton, Virginia*. Richmond, VA: Thomas R. Gray, 1831.

GREELEY, HORACE (ed.). *The Writings of Cassius Marcellus Clay*. New York, NY: Harper and Brothers, 1848.

——. *A History of the Struggle for Slavery Extension or Restriction in the United States From the Declaration of Independence to the Present Day*. New York, NY: Dix, Edwards and Co., 1856.

——. *The American Conflict: A History of the Great Rebellion in the United States, 1861-1865*. 2 vols. Hartford, CT: O. D. Case and Co., 1867.

GREENBERG, MARTIN H., and CHARLES G. WAUGH (eds.). *The Price of Freedom: Slavery and the Civil War - Vol. 1: The Demise of Slavery*. Nashville, TN: Cumberland House, 2000.

GRISSOM, MICHAEL ANDREW. *Southern By the Grace of God*. 1988. Gretna, LA: Pelican Publishing Co., 1995 ed.

HACKER, LOUIS MORTON. *The Shaping of the American Tradition*. New York, NY: Columbia University Press, 1947.

HAMILTON, ALEXANDER, JAMES MADISON, and JOHN JAY. *The Federalist: A Collection of Essays by Alexander Hamilton, James Madison, and John Jay*. New York, NY: The Co-operative Publication Society, 1901.

HENTY, GEORGE ALFRED. *Queen Victoria: Scenes From her Life and Reign*. London, UK: Blackie and Son, 1901.

HILDRETH, RICHARD. *The White Slave: Another Picture of Slave Life in America*. Boston, MA: Adamant Media Corp., 2001.

HINKLE, DON. *Embattled Banner: A Reasonable Defense of the Confederate Battle Flag*. Paducah, KY: Turner Publishing Co., 1997.

HOFFMAN, MICHAEL A., II. *They Were White and They Were Slaves: The Untold History of the Enslavement of Whites in Early America*. Dresden, NY: Wiswell Ruffin House, 1993.

HOFSTADTER, RICHARD. *The American Political Tradition, and the Men Who Made It*. New York, NY: Alfred A. Knopf, 1948.

——. (ed.) *Great Issues in American History: From Reconstruction to the Present Day, 1864-1969*. 1958. New York, NY: Vintage, 1969 ed.

HOLZER, HAROLD (ed.). *The Lincoln-Douglas Debates: The First Complete, Unexpurgated Text*. 1993. Bronx, NY: Fordham University Press, 2004 ed.

HORN, STANLEY F. *Invisible Empire: The Story of the Ku Klux Klan, 1866-1871*. 1939. Montclair, NJ: Patterson Smith, 1969 ed.

——. *The Decisive Battle of Nashville*. 1956. Baton Rouge, LA: Louisiana State University Press, 1991 ed.

HOSMER, JAMES K. *Samuel Adams*. 1885. Boston, MA: Houghton Mifflin Co., 1913 ed.

HURMENCE, BELINDA (ed.). *Before Freedom, When I Can Just Remember: Twenty-seven Oral Histories of Former South Carolina Slaves*. 1989. Winston-Salem, NC: John F. Blair, 2002 ed.

HUXLEY, LEONARD. *Life and Letters of Thomas Henry Huxley*. 3 vols. London, UK: Macmillan and Co., 1913.

JEFFERSON, THOMAS. *The Life and Morals of Jesus of Nazareth*. 1803. St. Louis, MO: N. D. Thompson, 1902 ed.

JENSEN, MERRILL. *The New Nation: A History of the United States During the Confederation, 1781-1789*. New York, NY: Vintage, 1950.

——. *The Articles of Confederation: An Interpretation of the Social-Constitutional History of the American Revolution, 1774-1781*. Madison, WI: University of Wisconsin Press, 1959.

JOHANNSEN, ROBERT WALTER. *Lincoln, the South, and Slavery: The Political Dimension*. Baton Rouge, LA: Louisiana State University Press, 1991.

JOHNSON, CLINT. *The Politically Incorrect Guide to the South (and Why It Will Rise Again)*. Washington, D.C.: Regnery, 2006.

JOHNSTONE, HUGER WILLIAM. *Truth of War Conspiracy, 1861*. Idylwild, GA: H. W. Johnstone, 1921.

JONES, JOHN WILLIAM. *The Davis Memorial Volume; Or Our Dead President, Jefferson Davis and the World's Tribute to His Memory*. Richmond, VA: B. F. Johnson, 1889.

JORDAN, DON, and MICHAEL WALSH. *White Cargo: The Forgotten History of Britain's White Slaves in America*. New York, NY: New York University Press, 2008.

KATCHER, PHILIP. *The Civil War Source Book*. 1992. New York, NY: Facts on File, 1995 ed.

——. *Brassey's Almanac: The American Civil War*. London, UK: Brassey's, 2003.

KECKLEY, ELIZABETH. *Behind the Scenes; or Thirty Years a Slave, and Four Years in the White House*. New York, NY: G. W. Carlton and Co., 1868.

KENNEDY, WILLIAM SLOANE. *Reminiscences of Walt Whitman, With Extracts From His Letters and Remarks on His Writings*. London, UK: Alexander Gardner, 1896.

KENNETT, LEE B. *Sherman: A Soldier's Life*. 2001. New York, NY: HarperCollins, 2002 ed.

LAMON, WARD HILL. *The Life of Abraham Lincoln: From His Birth to His Inauguration as President*. Boston, MA: James R. Osgood and Co., 1872.

——. *Recollections of Abraham Lincoln: 1847-1865*. Chicago, IL: A. C. McClurg and Co., 1895.

LANCASTER, BRUCE, and J. H. PLUMB. *The American Heritage Book of the Revolution*. 1958. New York, NY: Dell, 1975 ed.

LIVERMORE, THOMAS L. *Numbers and Losses in the Civil War in America, 1861-65. 1900*. Carlisle, PA: John Kallmann, 1996 ed.

MACKAY, CHARLES. *Life and Liberty in America, or Sketches of a Tour in the United States and Canada in 1857-58*. New York, NY: Harper and Brothers, 1859.

MACY, JESSE. *Political Parties in the United States, 1846-1861*. London, UK: Macmillan 1900.

MADISON, JAMES. *Letters and Other Writings of James Madison, Fourth President of the United States*. 4 vols. Philadelphia, PA: J. B. Lippincott and Co., 1865.

MAGLIOCCA, GERARD N. *The Tragedy of William Jennings Bryan: Constitutional Law and the Politics of Backlash*. New Haven, CT: Yale University Press, 2011.

MCCARTY, BURKE (ed.). *Little Sermons in Socialism by Abraham Lincoln*. Chicago, IL: The Chicago Daily Socialist, 1910.

MCKISSACK, PATRICIA C., and FREDERICK MCKISSACK. *Sojourner Truth: Ain't I a Woman?* New York: NY: Scholastic, 1992.

MCMANUS, EDGAR J. *A History of Negro Slavery in New York*. Syracuse, NY: Syracuse University Press, 1966.

MCPHERSON, JAMES M. *Battle Cry of Freedom: The Civil War Era*. New York, NY: Oxford University Press, 1988.

——. *Abraham Lincoln and the Second American Revolution*. 1991. New York, NY: Oxford University Press, 1992 ed.

MERIWETHER, ELIZABETH AVERY (pseudonym, "George Edmonds"). *Facts and Falsehoods Concerning the War on the South, 1861-1865*. Memphis, TN: A. R. Taylor and Co., 1904.

M'GILCHRIST, JOHN. *Lord Palmerston: A Biography*. London, UK: George Routledge and Sons, 1865.

MILLER, RUSSELL. *The Adventures of Arthur Conan Doyle: A Biography*. New York, NY: Thomas Dunne Books, 2008.

Minutes of the Eighth Annual Meeting and Reunion of the United Confederate Veterans, Atlanta, GA, July 20-23, 1898. New Orleans, LA: United Confederate Veterans, 1907.

Minutes of the Ninth Annual Meeting and Reunion of the United Confederate Veterans, Charleston, SC, May 10-13, 1899. New Orleans, LA: United Confederate Veterans, 1907.

Minutes of the Twelfth Annual Meeting and Reunion of the United Confederate Veterans, Dallas, TX, April 22-25, 1902. New Orleans, LA: United Confederate Veterans, 1907.

MISH, FREDERICK C. (ed.). *Webster's Ninth New Collegiate Dictionary*. 1984. Springfield, MA: Merriam-Webster.

MOORE, FRANK. *American Eloquence: A Collection of Speeches and Addresses, by the Most Eminent Orators of America*. 2 vols. New York, NY: D. Appleton and Co., 1858.

——. (ed.). *The Rebellion Record: A Diary of American Events*. 12 vols. New York, NY: G. P. Putnam, 1861.

MOORE, GEORGE HENRY. *Notes on the History of Slavery in Massachusetts*. New York, NY: D. Appleton and Co., 1866.

MOORE, JOHN HENRY. *A Study in States Rights*. New York, NY: Neale Publishing Co., 1911.

MORGAN, EDMUND S. *The Birth of the Republic, 1763-1789*. 1956. Chicago, IL: University of Chicago Press, 1967 ed.

MORRIS, THOMAS D. *Free Men All: The Personal Liberty Laws of the North, 1780-1861*. Baltimore, MD: Johns Hopkins University Press, 1974.

MUNFORD, BEVERLEY BLAND. *Virginia's Attitude Toward Slavery and Secession*. Richmond, VA: self-published, 1909.

MURPHY, JIM. *A Savage Thunder: Antietam and the Bloody Road to Freedom*. New York, NY: Margaret K. McElderry, 2009.

MUZZEY, DAVID SAVILLE. *The United States of America: Vol. 1, To the Civil War*. Boston, MA: Ginn and Co., 1922.

——. *The American Adventure: Vol. 2, From the Civil War*. 1924. New York, NY: Harper and Brothers, 1927 ed.

NAPOLITANO, ANDREW P. *The Constitution in Exile: How the Federal Government has Seized Power by Rewriting the Supreme Law of the Land*. Nashville, TN: Nelson Current, 2006.

NEILSON, WILLIAM ALLAN (ed.). *Webster's Biographical Dictionary*. Springfield, MA: G. and C. Merriam Co., 1943.

NICOLAY, JOHN G., and JOHN HAY (eds.). *Abraham Lincoln: A History*. 10 vols. New York, NY: The Century Co., 1890.

——. *Complete Works of Abraham Lincoln*. 12 vols. 1894. New York, NY: Francis D. Tandy Co., 1905 ed.

——. *Abraham Lincoln: Complete Works*. 12 vols. 1894. New York, NY: The Century Co., 1907 ed.

OATES, STEPHEN B. *Abraham Lincoln: The Man Behind the Myths*. New York, NY: Meridian, 1984.

——. *The Approaching Fury: Voices of the Storm, 1820-1861*. New York, NY: Harper Perennial, 1998.

ORA (full title: *The War of the Rebellion: A Compilation of the Official Records of the Union and Confederate Armies*). 70 vols. Washington, DC: Government Printing Office, 1880.

ORN (full title: *Official Records of the Union and Confederate Navies in the War of the Rebellion*). 30 vols. Washington, DC: Government Printing Office, 1894.

OWSLEY, FRANK LAWRENCE. *King Cotton Diplomacy: Foreign Relations of the Confederate States of America*. 1931. Chicago, IL: University of Chicago Press, 1959 ed.

PARRY, MELANIE (ed.). *Chambers Biographical Dictionary*. 1897. Edinburgh, Scotland: Chambers Harrap, 1998 ed.

POLLARD, EDWARD A. *Southern History of the War*. 2 vols. in 1. New York, NY: Charles B. Richardson, 1866.

——. *The Lost Cause*. 1867. Chicago, IL: E. B. Treat, 1890 ed.

——. *The Lost Cause Regained*. New York, NY: G. W. Carlton and Co., 1868.

——. *Life of Jefferson Davis, With a Secret History of the Southern Confederacy, Gathered "Behind the Scenes in Richmond."* Philadelphia, PA: National Publishing Co., 1869.

QUARLES, BENJAMIN. *The Negro in the Civil War*. 1953. Cambridge, MA: Da Capo Press, 1988 ed.

RANDALL, HENRY STEPHENS. *The Life of Thomas Jefferson*. 3 vols. New York, NY: Derby and Jackson, 1858.

RANDALL, JAMES GARFIELD. *Lincoln: The Liberal Statesman*. New York, NY: Dodd, Mead and Co., 1947.

RANDALL, JAMES GARFIELD, and RICHARD N. CURRENT. *Lincoln the President: Last Full Measure*. 1955. Urbana, IL: University of Illinois Press, 2000 ed.

RAWLE, WILLIAM. *A View of the Constitution of the United States of America*. Philadelphia, PA: H. C. Carey and I. Lea, 1825.

RICHARDSON, JAMES DANIEL (ed.). *A Compilation of the Messages and Papers of the Confederacy*. 2 vols. Nashville, TN: United States Publishing Co., 1905.

ROBERTS, PAUL M. *United States History: Review Text*. 1966. New York, NY: Amsco School

Publications, 1970 ed.

ROGERS, WILLIAM P. *The Three Secession Movements in the United States: Samuel J. Tilden, the Democratic Candidate for Presidency; the Advisor, Aider and Abettor of the Great Secession Movement of 1860; and One of the Authors of the Infamous Resolution of 1864; His Claims as a Statesman and Reformer Considered.* Boston, MA: John Wilson and Son, 1876.

ROZWENC, EDWIN CHARLES (ed.). *The Causes of the American Civil War.* 1961. Lexington, MA: D. C. Heath and Co., 1972 ed.

ROVE, KARL. *The Triumph of William McKinley: Why the Election of 1896 Still Matters.* New York, NY: Simon and Schuster, 2015.

RUTHERFORD, MILDRED LEWIS. *Four Addresses.* Birmingham, AL: The Mildred Rutherford Historical Circle, 1916.

——. *A True Estimate of Abraham Lincoln and Vindication of the South.* N.p., n.d.

——. *Truths of History: A Fair, Unbiased, Impartial, Unprejudiced and Conscientious Study of History.* Athens, GA: n.p., 1920.

——. *The South Must Have Her Rightful Place In History.* Athens, GA: n.p., 1923.

SAGE, BERNARD JANIN. *The Republic of Republics: A Retrospect of our Century of Federal Liberty.* Philadelphia, PA: self-published, 1878.

SEABROOK, LOCHLAINN. *Carnton Plantation Ghost Stories: True Tales of the Unexplained from Tennessee's Most Haunted Civil War House!* 2005. Franklin, TN, 2016 ed.

——. *Nathan Bedford Forrest: Southern Hero, American Patriot.* 2007. Franklin, TN, 2010 ed.

——. *Abraham Lincoln: The Southern View.* 2007. Franklin, TN: Sea Raven Press, 2013 ed.

——. *The McGavocks of Carnton Plantation: A Southern History - Celebrating One of Dixie's Most Noble Confederate Families and Their Tennessee Home.* 2008. Franklin, TN, 2011ed.

——. *A Rebel Born: A Defense of Nathan Bedford Forrest.* 2010. Franklin, TN: Sea Raven Press, 2011 ed.

——. *A Rebel Born: The Screenplay* (for the film). 2011. Franklin, TN: Sea Raven Press.

——. *Everything You Were Taught About the Civil War is Wrong, Ask a Southerner!* 2010. Franklin, TN: Sea Raven Press, revised 2014 ed.

——. *The Quotable Jefferson Davis: Selections From the Writings and Speeches of the Confederacy's First President.* Franklin, TN: Sea Raven Press, 2011.

——. *The Quotable Robert E. Lee: Selections From the Writings and Speeches of the South's Most Beloved Civil War General.* Franklin, TN: Sea Raven Press, 2011 Sesquicentennial Civil War Edition.

——. *Lincolnology: The Real Abraham Lincoln Revealed In His Own Words.* Franklin, TN: Sea Raven Press, 2011.

——. *The Unquotable Abraham Lincoln: The President's Quotes They Don't Want You To Know!* Franklin, TN: Sea Raven Press, 2011.

——. *Honest Jeff and Dishonest Abe: A Southern Children's Guide to the Civil War.* Franklin, TN: Sea Raven Press, 2012.

——. *Encyclopedia of the Battle of Franklin - A Comprehensive Guide to the Conflict that Changed the Civil War.* Franklin, TN: Sea Raven Press, 2012.

——. *The Quotable Nathan Bedford Forrest: Selections From the Writings and Speeches of the Confederacy's Most Brilliant Cavalryman.* Spring Hill, TN: Sea Raven Press, 2012.

——. *Forrest! 99 Reasons to Love Nathan Bedford Forrest.* Spring Hill, TN: Sea Raven Press, 2012.

——. *Give 'Em Hell Boys! The Complete Military Correspondence of Nathan Bedford Forrest.* Spring Hill, TN: Sea Raven Press, 2012.

——. *The Constitution of the Confederate States of America Explained: A Clause-by-Clause Study of the South's Magna Carta.* Spring Hill, TN: Sea Raven Press, 2012 Sesquicentennial Civil War Edition.

——. *The Great Impersonator: 99 Reasons to Dislike Abraham Lincoln*. Spring Hill, TN: Sea Raven Press, 2012.

——. *The Old Rebel: Robert E. Lee As He Was Seen By His Contemporaries*. Spring Hill, TN: Sea Raven Press, 2012 Sesquicentennial Civil War Edition.

——. *The Quotable Stonewall Jackson: Selections From the Writings and Speeches of the South's Most Famous General*. Spring Hill, TN: Sea Raven Press, 2012 Sesquicentennial Civil War Edition.

——. *Saddle, Sword, and Gun: A Biography of Nathan Bedford Forrest for Teens*. Spring Hill, TN: Sea Raven Press, 2013.

——. *The Alexander H. Stephens Reader: Excerpts From the Works of a Confederate Founding Father*. Spring Hill, TN: Sea Raven Press, 2013.

——. *The Quotable Alexander H. Stephens: Selections From the Writings and Speeches of the Confederacy's First Vice President*. Spring Hill, TN: Sea Raven Press, 2013 Sesquicentennial Civil War Edition.

——. *Give This Book to a Yankee! A Southern Guide to the Civil War for Northerners*. Spring Hill, TN: Sea Raven Press, 2014.

——. *The Articles of Confederation Explained: A Clause-by-Clause Study of America's First Constitution*. Spring Hill, TN: Sea Raven Press, 2014.

——. *Confederate Blood and Treasure: An Interview With Lochlainn Seabrook*. Spring Hill, TN: Sea Raven Press, 2015.

——. *Nathan Bedford Forrest and the Battle of Fort Pillow: Yankee Myth, Confederate Fact*. Spring Hill, TN: Sea Raven Press, 2015.

——. *Everything You Were Taught About American Slavery War is Wrong, Ask a Southerner!* Spring Hill, TN: Sea Raven Press, 2015.

——. *Confederacy 101: Amazing Facts You Never Knew About America's Oldest Political Tradition*. Spring Hill, TN: Sea Raven Press, 2015.

——. *The Great Yankee Coverup: What the North Doesn't Want You to Know About Lincoln's War!* Spring Hill, TN: Sea Raven Press, 2015.

——. *Slavery 101: Amazing Facts You Never Knew About America's "Peculiar Institution."* Spring Hill, TN: Sea Raven Press, 2015.

——. *Confederate Flag Facts: What Every American Should Know About Dixie's Southern Cross*. Spring Hill, TN: Sea Raven Press, 2016.

——. *Nathan Bedford Forrest and the Ku Klux Klan: Yankee Myth, Confederate Fact*. Spring Hill, TN: Sea Raven Press, 2016.

——. *Seabrook's Bible Dictionary of Traditional and Mystical Christian Doctrines*. Spring Hill, TN: Sea Raven Press, 2016.

——. *Everything You Were Taught About African-Americans and the Civil War is Wrong, Ask a Southerner!* Spring Hill, TN: Sea Raven Press, 2016.

——. *Nathan Bedford Forrest and African-Americans: Yankee Myth, Confederate Fact*. Spring Hill, TN: Sea Raven Press, 2016.

——. *Women in Gray: A Tribute to the Ladies Who Supported the Southern Confederacy*. Spring Hill, TN: Sea Raven Press, 2016.

——. *Lincoln's War: The Real Cause, the Real Winner, the Real Loser*. Spring Hill, TN: Sea Raven Press, 2016.

——. *The Unholy Crusade: Lincoln's Legacy of Destruction in the American South*. Spring Hill, TN: Sea Raven Press, 2017.

——. *Abraham Lincoln Was a Liberal, Jefferson Davis Was a Conservative: The Missing Key to Understanding the American Civil War*. Spring Hill, TN: Sea Raven Press, 2017.

——. *All We Ask is to be Let Alone: The Southern Secession Fact Book*. Spring Hill, TN: Sea Raven

Press, 2017.

SHENKMAN, RICHARD, and KURT EDWARD REIGER. *One-Night Stands with American History: Odd, Amusing, and Little-Known Incidents*. 1980. New York, NY: Perennial, 2003 ed.

SIMPSON, LEWIS P. (ed.). *I'll Take My Stand: The South and the Agrarian Tradition*. 1930. Baton Rouge, LA: University of Louisiana Press, 1977 ed.

SMITH, MARK M. (ed.). *The Old South*. Oxford, UK: Blackwell Publishers, 2001.

SMITH, PAGE. *Trial by Fire: A People's History of the Civil War and Reconstruction*. New York, NY: McGraw-Hill, 1982.

SNAY, MITCHELL. *Horace Greeley and the Politics of Reform in Nineteenth-Century America*. Lanham, MD: Rowman and Littlefield, 2011.

SOBEL, ROBERT (ed.). *Biographical Directory of the United States Executive Branch, 1774-1898*. Westport, CT: Greenwood Press, 1990.

SOTHERAN, CHARLES. *Horace Greeley and Other Pioneers of American Socialism*. 1892. New York, NY: Mitchell Kennerley, 1915 ed.

STAMPP, KENNETH M. *The Peculiar Institution: Slavery in the Antebellum South*. New York, NY: Vintage, 1956.

STANFORD, PETER THOMAS. *The Tragedy of the Negro in America*. Boston, MA: published by author, 1898.

STEPHENS, ALEXANDER HAMILTON. *Speech of Mr. Stephens, of Georgia, on the War and Taxation*. Washington, D.C.: J and G. Gideon, 1848.

——. *Recollections of Alexander H. Stephens: His Diary Kept When a Prisoner at Fort Warren, Boston Harbour, 1865*. New York, NY: Doubleday, Page, and Co., 1910.

——. *A Constitutional View of the Late War Between the States; Its Causes, Character, Conduct and Results*. 2 vols. Philadelphia, PA: National Publishing, Co., 1868.

STONEBRAKER, J. CLARENCE. *The Unwritten South: Cause, Progress and Results of the Civil War - Relics of Hidden Truth After Forty Years*. Seventh ed., n.p., 1908.

TAGG, LARRY. *The Unpopular Mr. Lincoln: The Story of America's Most Reviled President*. New York, NY: Savas Beatie, 2009.

TARBELL, IDA MINERVA. *The Life of Abraham Lincoln*. 4 vols. New York, NY: Lincoln History Society, 1895-1900.

TATALOVICH, RAYMOND, and BYRON W. DAYNES. *Presidential Power in the United States*. Monterey, CA: Brooks/Cole, 1984.

THOMAS, EMORY M. *The Confederate Nation: 1861-1865*. New York, NY: Harper and Row, 1979.

THOMPSON, HOLLAND. *The New South: A Chronicle of Social and Industrial Evolution*. New Haven, CT: Yale University Press, 1920.

TOCQUEVILLE, ALEXIS DE. *Democracy in America*. 2 vols. 1836. New York, NY: D. Appleton and Co., 1904 ed.

TOURGEE, ALBION W. *A Fool's Errand By One of the Fools*. London, UK: George Routledge and Sons, 1883.

TRAUPMAN, JOHN C. *The New College Latin and English Dictionary*. 1966. New York, NY: Bantam, 1988 ed.

WHITMAN, WALT. *Specimen Days In America*. 1882. London, UK: Walter Scott, 1887 ed.

WOODS, THOMAS E., JR. *The Politically Incorrect Guide to American History*. Washington, D.C.: Regnery, 2004.

INDEX

MEET THE AUTHOR

LOCHLAINN SEABROOK, a neo-Victorian and world acclaimed man of letters, is a Kentucky Colonel and the winner of the prestigious Jefferson Davis Historical Gold Medal for his "masterpiece," *A Rebel Born: A Defense of Nathan Bedford Forrest.* A classic littérateur and an unreconstructed Southern historian, he is an award-winning author, Civil War scholar, Bible authority, the leading popularizer of American Civil War history, and a traditional Southern Agrarian of Scottish, English, Irish, Dutch, Welsh, German, and Italian extraction.

A child prodigy, Seabrook is today a true Renaissance Man whose occupational titles also include encyclopedist, lexicographer, musician, artist, graphic designer, genealogist, photographer, and award-winning poet. Also a songwriter and a screenwriter, he has a 40 year background in historical nonfiction writing and is a member of the Sons of Confederate Veterans, the Civil War Trust, and the National Grange.

Copyright ©
SEA RAVEN PRESS

Above, Colonel Lochlainn Seabrook, "the voice of the traditional South," award-winning Civil War scholar and unreconstructed Southern historian. America's most prolific and popular pro-South author, his many books have introduced hundreds of thousands to the truth about the War for Southern Independence. He coined the phrase "South-shaming" and holds the world's record for writing the most books on Nathan Bedford Forrest: nine.

Known to his many fans as the "voice of the traditional South," due to similarities in their writing styles, ideas, and literary works, Seabrook is also often referred to as the "new Shelby Foote," the "Southern Joseph Campbell," and the "American Robert Graves" (his English cousin). Seabrook coined the terms "South-shaming" and "Lincolnian liberalism," and holds the world's record for writing the most books on Nathan Bedford Forrest: nine. In addition, Seabrook is the first Civil War scholar to connect the early American nickname for the U.S., "The Confederate States of America," with the Southern Confederacy that arose eight decades later, and the first to note that in 1860 the party platforms of the two major political parties were the opposite of what they are today (Victorian Democrats were conservatives, Victorian Republicans were liberals).

The grandson of an Appalachian coal-mining family, Seabrook is a seventh-generation Kentuckian, co-chair of the Jent/Gent Family Committee (Kentucky), founder and director of the Blakeney Family Tree Project, and a board member of the Friends of Colonel Benjamin E. Caudill. Seabrook's literary works have been endorsed by leading authorities, museum curators, award-winning historians, bestselling authors, celebrities, noted scientists, well regarded educators, TV show hosts and producers, renowned military artists, esteemed Southern organizations, and distinguished academicians from around the world.

Seabrook has authored over 50 popular adult books on the American Civil War, American and international slavery, the U.S. Confederacy (1781), the Southern Confederacy (1861), religion, theology, thealogy, Jesus, the Bible, the Apocrypha, the Law of Attraction, alternative health, spirituality, ghost stories, the paranormal, ufology, social issues, and cross-cultural studies of the family and marriage. His Confederate biographies, pro-South studies, genealogical monographs, family histories, military encyclopedias, self-help guides, and etymological dictionaries have received wide acclaim.

Seabrook's eight children's books include a Southern guide to the Civil War, a biography of Nathan Bedford Forrest, a dictionary of religion and myth, a rewriting of the King Arthur legend (which reinstates the original pre-Christian motifs), two bedtime stories for preschoolers, a naturalist's guidebook to owls, a worldwide look at the family, and an examination of the Near-Death Experience.

Of blue-blooded Southern stock through his Kentucky, Tennessee, Virginia, West Virginia, and North Carolina ancestors, he is a direct descendant of European royalty via his 6th great-grandfather, the Earl of Oxford, after which London's famous Harley Street is named. Among his celebrated male Celtic ancestors is Robert the Bruce, King of Scotland, Seabrook's 22nd great-grandfather. The 21st great-grandson of Edward I "Longshanks" Plantagenet), King of England, Seabrook is a thirteenth-generation Southerner through his descent from the colonists of Jamestown, Virginia (1607).

(Photo © Lochlainn Seabrook)

The 2nd, 3rd, and 4th great-grandson of dozens of Confederate soldiers, one of his closest connections to Lincoln's War is through his 3rd great-grandfather, Elias Jent, Sr., who fought for the Confederacy in the Thirteenth Cavalry Kentucky under Seabrook's 2nd cousin, Colonel Benjamin E. Caudill. The Thirteenth, also known as "Caudill's Army," fought in numerous conflicts, including the Battles of Saltville, Gladsville, Mill Cliff, Poor Fork, Whitesburg, and Leatherwood.

Seabrook is a direct descendant of the families of Alexander H. Stephens, John Singleton Mosby, William Giles Harding, and Edmund Winchester Rucker, and is related to the following Confederates and other 18th- and 19th-Century luminaries: Robert E. Lee, Stephen Dill Lee, Stonewall Jackson, Nathan Bedford Forrest, James Longstreet, John Hunt Morgan, Jeb Stuart, Pierre G. T. Beauregard (approved the Confederate Battle Flag design), George W. Gordon, John Bell Hood, Alexander Peter Stewart, Arthur M. Manigault, Joseph Manigault, Charles Scott Venable, Thornton A. Washington, John A. Washington, Abraham Buford, Edmund W. Pettus, Theodrick "Tod" Carter, John B. Womack, John H. Winder, Gideon J. Pillow, States Rights Gist, Henry R. Jackson, John Lawton Seabrook, John C. Breckinridge, Leonidas Polk, Zachary Taylor, Sarah Knox Taylor (first wife of Jefferson Davis), Richard Taylor, Davy Crockett, Daniel Boone, Meriwether Lewis (of the Lewis and Clark Expedition)

 Andrew Jackson, James K. Polk, Abram Poindexter Maury (founder of Franklin, TN), Zebulon Vance, Thomas Jefferson, Edmund Jennings Randolph, George Wythe Randolph (grandson of Jefferson), Felix K. Zollicoffer, Fitzhugh Lee, Nathaniel F. Cheairs, Jesse James, Frank James, Robert Brank Vance, Charles Sidney Winder, John W. McGavock, Caroline E. (Winder) McGavock, David Harding McGavock, Lysander McGavock, James Randal McGavock, Randal William McGavock, Francis McGavock, Emily McGavock, William Henry F. Lee, Lucius E. Polk, Minor Meriwether (husband of noted pro-South author Elizabeth Avery Meriwether), Ellen Bourne Tynes (wife of Forrest's chief of artillery, Captain John W. Morton), South Carolina Senators Preston Smith Brooks and Andrew Pickens Butler, and famed South Carolina diarist Mary Chesnut.

Seabrook's modern day cousins include: Patrick J. Buchanan (conservative author), Cindy Crawford (model), Shelby Lee Adams (Letcher Co., Kentucky, photographer), Bertram Thomas Combs (Kentucky's 50th governor), Edith Bolling (wife of President Woodrow Wilson), and actors Andy Griffith, Riley Keough, George C. Scott, Robert Duvall, Reese Witherspoon, Lee Marvin, Rebecca Gayheart, and Tom Cruise.

Seabrook's screenplay, *A Rebel Born*, based on his book of the same name, has been signed with acclaimed filmmaker Christopher Forbes (of Forbes Film). It is now in pre-production, and is set for release in 2017 as a full-length feature film. This will be the first movie ever made of Nathan Bedford Forrest's life story, and as a historically accurate project written from the Southern perspective, is destined to be one of the most talked about Civil War films of all time.

Born with music in his blood, Seabrook is an award-winning, multi-genre, BMI-Nashville songwriter and lyricist who has composed some 3,000 songs (250 albums), and whose original music has been heard in film (*A Rebel Born, Cowgirls 'n Angels, Confederate Cavalry, Billy the Kid: Showdown in Lincoln County, Vengeance Without Mercy, Last Step, County Line, The Mark*) and on TV and radio worldwide. A musician, producer, multi-instrumentalist, and renown performer—whose keyboard work has been variously compared to pianists from Hargus Robbins and Vince Guaraldi to Elton John and Leonard Bernstein—Seabrook has opened for groups such as the Earl Scruggs Review, Ted Nugent, and Bob Seger, and has performed privately for such public figures as President Ronald Reagan, Burt Reynolds, Loni Anderson, and Senator Edward W. Brooke. Seabrook's cousins in the music business include: Johnny Cash, Elvis Presley, Lisa Marie Presley, Billy Ray and Miley Cyrus, Patty Loveless, Tim McGraw, Lee Ann Womack, Dolly Parton, Pat Boone, Naomi, Wynonna, and Ashley Judd, Ricky Skaggs, the Sunshine Sisters, Martha Carson, and Chet Atkins.

Seabrook lives with his wife and family in historic Middle Tennessee, the heart of Forrest country and the Confederacy, where his conservative Southern ancestors fought valiantly against Liberal Lincoln and the progressive North in defense of Jeffersonianism, constitutional government, and personal liberty.

If you enjoyed this book you will be interested in Colonel Seabrook's other popular related titles:

☛ EVERYTHING YOU WERE TAUGHT ABOUT THE CIVIL WAR IS WRONG, ASK A SOUTHERNER!
☛ ABRAHAM LINCOLN WAS A LIBERAL, JEFFERSON DAVIS WAS A CONSERVATIVE
☛ ALL WE ASK IS TO BE LET ALONE: THE SOUTHERN SECESSION FACT BOOK
☛ EVERYTHING YOU WERE TAUGHT ABOUT AMERICAN SLAVERY IS WRONG, ASK A SOUTHERNER!
☛ CONFEDERATE FLAG FACTS: WHAT EVERY AMERICAN SHOULD KNOW ABOUT DIXIE'S SOUTHERN CROSS
☛ LINCOLN'S WAR: THE REAL CAUSE, THE REAL WINNER, THE REAL LOSER

Available from Sea Raven Press and wherever fine books are sold

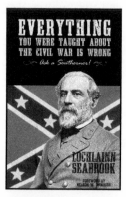

ALL OF OUR BOOK COVERS ARE AVAILABLE AS 11" X 17" POSTERS, SUITABLE FOR FRAMING

SeaRavenPress.com • NathanBedfordForrestBooks.com

CPSIA information can be obtained
at www.ICGtesting.com
Printed in the USA
FFHW020459150219
50559720-55875FF

9 781943 737512